Strictly Come Dancing

The Official
2009 Annual

Alison Maloney

BBC
BOOKS

This book is published to accompany the
television series *Strictly Come Dancing*,
first broadcast on BBC1 in 2008.

10 9 8 7 6 5 4 3 2 1

Published in 2008 by BBC Books,
an imprint of Ebury Publishing,
A Random House Group Company.

Foreword by Bruce Forsyth and Tess Daly
Copyright © Woodlands Books Limited 2008
Main text by Alison Maloney
Copyright © Woodlands Books Limited 2008

BBC Books would like to thank Sam Donnelly, Helen Bishop and the
rest of the *Strictly Come Dancing* production team for all their help
in compiling this book.

Alison Maloney has asserted her right to be identified as the author of this
Work in accordance with the Copyright, Designs and Patents Act 1988

The Random House Group Limited Reg. No. 954009

Addresses for companies within the Random House Group can be found at
www.randomhouse.co.uk

A CIP catalogue record for this book is available
from the British Library.

ISBN 978 1 846 07611 4

The Random House Group Limited makes every effort to ensure that the
papers used in our books are made from trees that have been legally
sourced from well-managed and credibly certified forests. Our paper
procurement policy can be found on www.randomhouse.co.uk

Commissioning editor: Lorna Russell
Project editors: Eleanor Maxfield and Laura Higginson
Designer: Bobby Birchall, Bobby&Co
Production: Helen Everson

Colour origination, printing and binding by Butler, Tanner & Dennis Ltd

Picture credits:

Page 3 (curtain), p.20 (male dancing shoes – both duplicated on other
pages) © istockphoto.com; p.5 (disco ball background), p.10 (light effect),
p.16 (gold disco ball), p.22 (female dancing shoes), p.30 (disco ball
background), p.74 (pink fabric – all duplicated on other pages)
© dreamstime.com
Series six photography by David Venni © BBC
Series five photography by Greg King, Mark Chilvers, Todd Anthony,
Kieron McCarron, Emma Campbell, David Venni and Abi Wyles © BBC
Strictly Come Dancing Tour photography © Alfie Hitchcock
Dancersize photography by Greg King © BBC Woodlands Ltd
Pages 36–7 photographs of Hélio Castroneves © Steve C.
Mitchell/epa/Corbis; Monica Seles © Joshua Lott/Reuters/Corbis; Priscilla
Presley © Jon Kopaloff/FilmMagic/Getty Images

Contents

Foreword
Bruce Forsyth

Wow! We did it again. Series five was incredible thanks to a lot of talented dancers, both professional and amateur. The truth is, with a show as popular as *Strictly Come Dancing*, you never know how it's going to go, but then you have a fifth series that tops the other four, which is quite unbelievable.

The calibre of contestants is mainly due to the people who work so hard behind the scenes, who rarely get a mention. We must never forget the researchers and the production team who find the celebrities. They do a fantastic job of getting the right people, and the right mix.

To get Kelly Brook, who was so magnificent, and Gabby Logan, who is a wonderful gymnast and one of the favourites at the start, was fantastic – didn't they do well! Oh, sorry, I wasn't going to say that!

Alesha Dixon was a revelation because she came from a poor home where she couldn't go to dancing lessons, although she desperately wanted to dance. On *Strictly* she got the chance to learn after all these years and she is now a qualified dancer and could front any line-up anywhere, even in Las Vegas. She is now an incredible dancing performer as well as being a singer. What a wonderful thing to find out.

Every year the research team also find a couple who are not so young, which always creates interest. I'll never forget Jimmy Tarbuck, who had to drop out due to ill health. I was reading something recently where he said, 'I should never have gone into it.' The trouble was, in the second week they were doing a hip-hop jitterbug group dance that was the wrong dance for him even to attempt. Poor Jimmy, he had a very funny tango outfit, which we never got to see.

Strictly goes from strength to strength because the celebrities look at the show themselves and say, 'Ooh, I'd love to have a go at that.' To get celebrities on the first series was more than difficult but since then everyone wants to have a go.

Anyone can do it, as long as people have control of their limbs, can walk with a bit of rhythm and move their arms. This is why sportsmen and sportswomen are so good – they have control of their limbs, they are disciplined and they have a competitive edge. Darren Gough, for example, couldn't dance at all in the first and second week, and we thought, He's not going to last long. And then he went and won it.

This series saw so many good dancers coming through at the end so, for the last four or five weeks, we really didn't know who would be the winner. The show can be so unpredictable – take the quarter-finals when Matt had his terrible wobble. It takes a lot of guts to go out there in front of a live audience and do a routine. They put a lot of time into it and the professionals do a wonderful job training them, but they still have the live performance on top of that. It's a mental and physical nightmare for a lot of them so they deserve sympathy when they lose their nerve.

I felt very sorry for Matt that night, as did everybody. We could only smile at him, give him a pat on the back and say, 'You'll be fine next week.' Luckily the public kept him in so he could have another go, and he did really well.

This year will be my first series as an octogenarian. My 80th birthday, in February, was the worst-kept secret ever and I had a fantastic night making the BBC show *Happy Birthday, Brucie*. It gave me the rare chance to work with many different people: I did a piano duet with Jools Holland, a tap dance with the boys from *Billy Elliot* and I even had a chance to sing a straight song at the end. You see, I'm still a variety performer but I don't often get the chance to do all that these days so it was a real Brucie bonus.

I also got to turn the tables on the *Strictly* judges. They had to ice a cake and I got to be the judge. Len was propping his up until the last minute, when it finally fell over, and Arlene kept giggling all the time – she's a lovely choreographer but she can't choreograph cakes. Craig's effort was a complete mess, which everybody was thrilled about!

With each series of *Strictly Come Dancing*, I look forward to it more because the standard of the dancing just gets better and better all the time. Series six does have a lot to live up to, so I can't wait to see what happens.

Tess Daly

Strictly Come Dancing continues to go from strength to strength and series five was our most exciting and dynamic series yet. The standard of dancing exceeded anything we've seen before and the contestants were so engaging and so much fun. Backstage, they all got on like a house on fire and the party atmosphere was contagious.

We saw a huge glamour injection in series five, with a lot of very sexy ladies, meaning that there was a whole new audience of male viewers who had never watched the show before. Mind you, there were some cute chaps too – let's not leave the lady viewers out of it!

I was excited to see Stephanie Beacham's name when the list of new celebrities was announced. I was desperate to meet her. I'd interviewed her before and she is a diva, but a warm-hearted one. She's witty, full of one-liners and fabulous through and through. There's never a dull moment when Stephanie's around so we were all devastated when she was one of the first to leave. We all adored her.

With Penny Lancaster-Stewart competing, I also got to meet Rod Stewart and he's great. He's very rock 'n' roll – the ultimate rock star – and he doesn't disappoint. He was very supportive of Penny and came to see her dance almost every week.

As always, the contestants worked their socks off and different people impressed me at different stages of the competition. Letitia Dean suddenly turned a corner and emerged as this graceful ballroom dancer. The judges mentioned her posture and she worked on it, and she was so much better for it. She had amazing commitment.

Kenny blew me away with his personality – and with his kilt! He was great to be around and we all loved him to bits. He was like the team leader, a big-brother type, who kept an eye on the young guns like Matt Di Angelo and Gethin Jones. They really looked up to him, calling him Big Daddy.

Alesha astounded me with her dancing and

her exuberance – it was so mesmerizing to watch – and Kate impressed me because she was just so much fun. She gave her all, even though sadly it wasn't enough. She took a lot of knocks but the audience got behind her because she's a lovely lady and they could see she was trying her best.

It was really sad to see Gabby go so early. The whole nation was talking about the Gabby controversy, when she was left in the bottom two with Penny despite great scores from the judges. It was on the news and it was even on the pin-board at my daughter's pre-school! She could have been incredible and it was a shame because she was so thrilled to be a part of the show and she was loving the costumes. It was devastating to see how disappointed and bewildered by the vote she was.

John Barnes is gorgeous, like a big, cuddly teddy bear, and he was always giving us all bear hugs. They were all a great bunch. There were no bad eggs, no egos – they were all in it together. Even Brendan was good tempered, although I do quite welcome a Brendan strop because it adds drama. This year I think he was rather overcome by his partner, the stunning Kelly Brook. He was wowed into submission.

It was a terrible shame that Kelly had to drop out because of the loss of her father. Who knows how far she would have gone but she felt she couldn't carry on and we could only support her.

The dance off, introduced for series five, added an extra dynamic to the show. The judges now have the final word, which is supposed to stop the wrong dancer going out and it becoming a popularity contest. It should be about dancing ability and we thought it would be fairer on the contestants – although it didn't save poor Gabby. The dance off adds drama because it's a cliffhanger. It doesn't matter how well the couples danced in the first part of the show; it has to be judged on the repeat performance, so they have to try not to fall apart, keep a tight grip on the nerves and dance their hearts out. The audience were on the edge of their seats, as were we, and we had more viewers than we've ever had before so obviously people at home enjoyed it as much as we did.

The incredible standard in series five was largely down to the tremendous hard work of the celebrities. Couples put in more hours of training than previous seasons. They were very serious about the competition and we'd never seen that level of commitment before. But, in this contest, the more you train the better you get.

The final between Matt Di Angelo and Alesha Dixon was incredibly close. They both had a huge amount of ability and were equally popular, so none of us knew which way it was going to go. It made for a thrilling climax to the show.

In my house, *Strictly Come Dancing* is a family affair. Vernon is an avid fan and for series five our daughter, Phoebe, really got the whole concept of the show. She was only three years old and she'll be four just before this series but she was completely hooked. Every morning she asked me if she could wear her '*Strictly Come Dancing* dress', a party dress with a swirly skirt with a little bit of sparkle on it. Then she'd put on her best sparkly shoes and hum the theme tune all day. She was completely enthralled.

As a treat we brought Phoebe to watch during the rehearsals. She was completely mesmerized by everyone – because she'd seen them on TV, she thought she knew them.

Phoebe's been talking about the next series ever since the last one ended and I feel the same – I can't wait for series six. It's a longer run this year, with two more contestants. It's the highlight of my year so, as far as I'm concerned, the more the merrier!

A is for Arguments

Tiffs in the training room are all too common as the frustration and fatigue sets in. Georgina Bouzova and James Jordan were frequently fighting in series four, cheeky chappy Dominic Littlewood lost his temper with Lilia Kopylova in series five and even perfect partners Matt and Flavia had a falling out along the way. But the most frequent spats are among the judges, who bickered their way through numerous issues in series five. In show one Len commented, 'I think Craig's bow-tie is too tight and the blood's gone to his brain' and it was all downhill from there!

B is for Bottoms

Derrieres were the talk of series five. First Gethin described his first meeting with dance partner Camilla, saying, 'You meet this gorgeous Danish dancer and the first thing she says is, "Put your hand on my bum!" Weird.' Then head judge Len Goodman accused Dominic Littlewood of being a 'bumwatcher'. 'D'you know what gets on my nerves,' he declared. 'Every time you're behind Lilia, why are you studying her bum? Bumwatcher!' After the dance Lilia asked Dominic, 'How was my bum?' to which the cheeky chappy replied, 'Your bum was lovely.'

C is for Children

Knowing his audience well, Bruce likes to mention the children in his introduction every Saturday night. Not only has the show proved a great hit with young people, it has also provided much-needed cash to help disadvantaged children. Every vote raises 12.5p for Children in Need and series five raised a whopping £1,033,097.

D is for Dance Off

Series five saw a change in the format as the bottom two couples in each show found themselves in a dance off for the first time. They would then perform their dance for a second time and it was the judges' decision who to eliminate, with Len having the casting vote in a tie. Designed to prevent a great dancer being knocked out while other, more popular contestants stayed, it still caused drama, and frustration for the judges, when Penny and Gabby came head to head, forcing Len to choose between them.

E is for EastEnders

Since Christopher Parker first took to the floor the show has been a favourite of the *EastEnders* cast. The last three series saw Jill Halfpenny, Patsy Palmer and Louisa Lytton strut their stuff and series five had two *EastEnders*, in the form of the elegant Letitia Dean and the dashing Matt Di Angelo. The studio audience was packed with Albert Square residents too, including Kellie Shirley, Barbara Windsor and Matt's screen mum, Linda Henry.

F is for Feet

The first thing that the celebrity dancers get out of their intensive training is very sore feet! For most it means blisters and bruises but for the unfortunate few it can be more serious. Colin Jackson ended up in casualty with a severely bruised toe, Bill

Turnbull hobbled on for weeks with a nasty ankle injury and Kate Garraway began series five on crutches after damaging both her tendons.

G is for Gymnastics

Former gymnastics champion Gabby Logan wowed the crowd with some stunning moves in her dances. Her Samba had a backwards walkover and her jive contained a cartwheel, which finished in the splits. Judge Craig Revel Horwood loved it: 'The cartwheel and splits – I think you are a star!' he said.

H is for Hollywood

Hollywood came to Shepherd's Bush in October, with the glamorous leading ladies Stephanie Beacham and Kelly Brook dancing up a storm and *Titanic* star Billy Zane turning up every Saturday to cheer Kelly on.

I is for Illness

In every series, some of the contestants are suffering more than the usual muscle strain, as they battle through viruses and bugs to make it through Saturday night. Zoe Ball fought the flu to bring us her series three cha-cha-cha, Brian Capron's first-round waltz suffered the same fate and put him out of the competition, Letitia Dean succumbed to a sickness bug that was going around in week nine of series five, and had to perform two dances for the first time – in between being sick.

J is for Jibes

Bruce is always charming to the contestants but he can never resist a dig at the judges. He introduced them on the first show of series five with the words, 'Our four esteemed judges, whose names we could never forget – Craig Revel Horrid, Arlene Fusspot, Len Goodmoan and Bruno Mussolini.' In the semi-final, he quipped, 'Alesha is the last girl in the competition. She said, "Bruce I feel so lonely. I have no one to have a girly gossip with, no one to share make-up tips with and no one to have a good old natter with over a cup of tea." I said, "Have you tried Craig?"'

K is for Kilt

It took five series for the first kilt to appear on *Strictly Come Dancing*, thanks to patriotic Scot Kenny Logan. His unforgettable paso doble saw him whip off a cape to reveal a black and gold kilt. It ended with Ola underneath his outstretched legs, covering her eyes to protect his modesty.

L is for Legs

In the Latin section the ladies' legs are revealed in their full glory, and this year there was more leg than usual, especially in the case of Penny Lancaster-Stewart. Rod Stewart's photographer wife boasts a pair of pins with an inside leg measurement of 36 inches. Hot legs indeed!

M is for Make-up

An integral part of every dancer's ensemble, the make-up and hair takes hours to create. Stylist Sarah Burrows and her team spend all week designing the look and, on Saturday, will begin styling the ladies first thing in the morning. For the celebrities, though, the make-up chair can provide a welcome respite. 'It's the only time of the day when they get to sit down and relax,' says Sarah. 'It's like having a massage. They shut their eyes and think about what's happened during the week, so you build up quite a close relationship. Normally you can't get them out!'

N is for Nan

Or in Alesha Dixon's case, two of them. The singer's two grandmothers were her most fervent supporters, cheering her on each week and even organising a mini tea dance to get her in the mood for her ballroom dances. Her week five foxtrot had Nan Clem in tears and the semi-finals saw proud, Maureen dabbing at her eyes. After getting 36 points for her week-three jive Alesha joked, 'I knew when I got the nines my family would be bouncing off the walls. My nan says she is going to charge the BBC for the damage to her ceiling.'

O is for Ovations

A standing ovation from the judges is a rare and precious thing. Gabby Logan received one when she lost the dance off in show four and Penny Lancaster-Stewart got the same treatment two weeks later. Len gave Matt a one-man ovation in the semi-finals for his waltz. 'They all deserved a standing ovation from me but with the added pressure that Matt had after last week [see Q], I thought he came out and did the most marvellous waltz.'

P is for The Perils of Pauline

After Kate Garraway managed to get through to week seven, Len Goodman summed her up with one of his fabulous stories. 'I used to go to Saturday-morning cinema and there was a show called *The Perils of Pauline*,' he explained. 'Every week she ended up in a disastrous situation and every week you thought, She's never coming back. But every week – back she comes!'

Q is for Quarter-finals

By the time the contestants get to the quarter-finals, the pressure is really on. For poor Matt Di Angelo it proved too much and his routines suffered. First the foxtrot fell apart, then the evening went from bad to worse, when he completely forgot the samba halfway through.

R is for Rules

You can't have a dance competition without rules but, for some, rules are there to be broken. Brendan Cole has yet to get through a series without at least one illegal lift. His magnificent rumba with Claire King, in series four, won high praise from Bruno and Craig but was marked down due to a lift – with Arlene giving them a 'furious four!' His American Smooth with Kelly Brook caused controversy when Bruno gave them a ten, despite an illegal third lift, and Len called Brendan 'A rebel without a clue' and 'a dozy pillock'.

S is for Sparkle

The set, the dresses, the shoes and even the trophy just wouldn't be the same without a bit of razzle-dazzle. From Brendan's pink jive shoes to Penny's shimmering samba dress, each outfit is lovingly created to give maximum sparkle. The outfits are often decorated with hundreds of Swarovski crystals, each sewn on by hand. To date over three million crystals have been used on the show.

T is for Tens

For a *Strictly* contestant, there's only one thing more thrilling than landing a perfect ten – and that's getting all four of them. Series five saw all records smashed by Alesha Dixon and Matthew Cutler, who managed a whopping 19 top scores, although maximum points eluded her. However, runner-up Matt Di Angelo's became the third person awarded 40 points with his magnificent semi-final waltz, following in the footsteps of previous winners Mark Ramprakash and Jill Halfpenny.

U is for Undies

After a picture of Len in his dressing gown appeared in the papers, Bruce brought a blush to Bruno's cheeks when he produced a photo of the Italian judge posing in his pants as a young man. Elsewhere, lucky underwear was the order of the day. Letitia had a pair of lucky knickers. Kenny was even wearing lucky pants when he did his paso doble – so now you know what a Scotsman wears under his kilt.

V is for Variety

As well as the differences in the dancing – and the ability of the dancers – the show gives viewers the chance to see a variety of different performers. From our own dear Brucie, with

a classic big-band number, to R 'n' B star Beyoncé and Kylie Minogue, the show spans the gamut of musical taste. Series five saw such diverse acts as Welsh diva Katherine Jenkins, balladeer James Blunt and boy band McFly. Something for everyone, indeed.

W is for Wife Swapping

Kenny and Gabby Logan were the first married couple to enter the contest so it was only right to team them up with *Strictly*'s own bride and groom, James and Ola Jordan. The rivalry was intense, with Kenny declaring, 'If I'm in a dance off with Gabby, I want to stay in and I want her to go out.' But, after Gabby's shock exit, she and James gave Kenny and Ola their full support.

X is for X-rated

Of course, it's a family show so it's always in the best-possible taste. But the series-five contestants raised the temperature in the studio with their tribute to *Dirty Dancing* on the twentieth anniversary of the film. Phew!

Y is for You

There's no show without an audience and every year millions of you tune in to cheer on our celebs. In fact, 12.09 million viewers watched as Alesha and Matt battled it out in the series-five final.

Z is for Zorbing

In what has to be the most creative dance training to date, Camilla took Gethin Jones Zorbing to help him cope with the giddiness he felt in the Viennese waltz. For those who don't know, that's rolling down a hill in a huge inflatable ball!

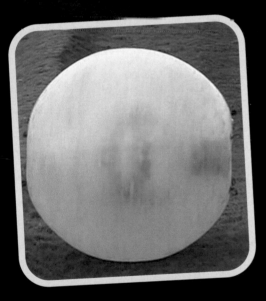

Andrew Castle

Andrew Castle is clearly a glutton for punishment. Having watched *GMTV* colleagues Fiona Phillips and Kate Garraway suffer through a series of disastrous dances and painful injuries, he decided it was his turn to try his luck on the dance floor!

He was persuaded by the two former contestants who assured him that it's the best thing they have ever done in their lives. He also rang Roger Black who said, 'You'll have the time of your life but you'll be utterly petrified!'

A former professional tennis player, the breakfast presenter considers himself to be quite fit, although he doesn't think that will give him an added advantage. He is,

Partner: Ola Jordan

however, a total dance novice. The only bit of real dancing he has ever had to do was the first dance on his wedding day – and his father-in-law had to teach him the moves.

Even then, Andrew confesses he felt vulnerable and nervous, performing a two-minute dance in front of all his family and his friends. He was desperately pleading with the guests to come and join them on the dance floor.

The father of two teenage daughters, Andrew refuses to dance even at parties and family weddings, for fear of being seen as an embarrassing dad. He does admit to the occasional bop around his living room when the girls were younger, but when it comes to ballroom and Latin, he is completely clueless. 'I'd have to look in the dictionary and find out which is which and what's listed underneath it!' he confesses.

'On my first day of training I was handed a pair of shiny shoes and a pair of heeled matt shoes and didn't have a clue which pair of shoes to put on for which dance.'

Knowing as little as he does, he is prepared for the odd scathing comment from the judges but, ever the gent, he hopes they will direct their criticism at him alone. 'It would be unfeasible if they didn't have some sort of a go at me,' he says. 'The only control I have is how much effort I put in each week. I'm being judged by world-class judges – I know nothing, they know everything! So it's fair enough.

'But if they criticize my partner, it's a different story and I may well step in and defend her.'

A big fan of the show, Andrew thinks he will have fun while competing, but will also bring something extra to his marriage to former air hostess Sophia. 'The idea of learning how to dance with a world-class partner is a once-in-a-lifetime opportunity,' he says. 'And I would love nothing more than being able to dance with my wife, and be quite good at it!'

The Story of Series Five
Dancing Divas and Dashing Dudes

1. Murder on the Dance Floor

Fourteen celebrities gathered once again for the beginning of an epic journey. Among them a Hollywood legend, two stunning models, a sprinkling of sportsmen, a couple of *EastEnders* and a serial killer! Brian Capron, who once terrorized the cobbles of *Coronation Street*, was himself cruelly axed in the very first dance off. And he managed to bring down last year's winning dancer, Karen Hardy, with a waltz that, according to Bruno, came from 'six feet under'.

2. Take My Wife …

Programme one also introduced the first married celebrities to compete on *Strictly*, in the impressive forms of Kenny and Gabby Logan. Appropriately they were paired with married dancers Ola and James Jordan. But former gymnast Gabby and International Rugby player Kenny were soon demonstrating the competitive streak in the Logan household. 'If I say I've danced for four hours she'll say she's danced for five,' explained Kenny.

3. Len Behaving Badly

It didn't take long for the judges to get hot under the collar. Their first tiff of the season came after Gethin Jones and Camilla Dallerup performed cha-cha-cha that was, according to Craig, 'completely square' and 'lacked hip action'. A furious Len retorted, 'I think Craig's bow-tie is too tight and the blood's gone to his brain!' And when Bruno got himself into a lather about 'the action man running out of steam', and added, 'I'm sorry, I'm not happy. You have to do better,' Len told him, 'Don't get out of bed over it! Take a Valium and calm down!' Ouch.

4. Bar Rumba

Queen of the Vic Letitia Dean was clearly shaken when her rumba with Darren Bennett went down about as well as a flat pint with a punter. Craig's comment that 'It was all too clean and clinical. Really cold,' left her close to tears. And with a score of 23 she found herself in the dance off. Meanwhile, Kelly Brook made a sizzling start, prompting Len to tell her partner, Brendan Cole, 'You must think you've died and gone to heaven. I'm surprised the smoke detectors didn't go off.' Her rumba put her at the top of the table with Penny Lancaster-Stewart and Ian Waite.

5. Pain but No Gain

Kate Garraway got off to a terrible start after injuring both ankles before even performing her first dance. After being strapped up for the opening show, she battled on in show two, with a quickstep that left the judges flat. After scoring just 15, she said, 'I started off with two dodgy feet and I feel like my whole body has been mauled by the judges.' Then turning away from the camera she added, 'I want to cry.' Luckily, the public were on her side and she dodged the dreaded dance off.

6. The Diva Bows Out

Dynasty star Stephanie Beacham brought Hollywood to the dance floor with her elegant quickstep. Craig was impressed. 'You arrived with all the class in the world. It was fantastic. A very respectable attempt,' he told her. Later, he said the star had stood out in the programme because she was 'a real glamour queen'. However, the public disagreed and Stephanie was voted out in the dance off. Once more, she showed sheer class when she breathed a sigh of relief and said, 'Oh, thank goodness!'

Alesha and Matthew

Brian and Karen

Gabby and James

Dominic and Lilia

Kate and Anton

Gethin and Camilla

Kelly and Brendan

7. Leggy Logan

Former gymnast Gabby Logan proved she still has it with a spectacular jive that included a cartwheel and ended in the splits! The judges were gleeful. 'You got the party started,' said Bruno. Craig told her, 'I think you're a star,' and Arlene raved, 'You look like you googled jive, pressed the key and it all went into you. Fabulously done.' Sadly, she still managed to be outdone by Alesha Dixon and Matt Cutler, who scored the highest score so far when she landed 36 for a jive which Len called, 'Fun, fast, fantastic'.

8. Penny For Your Thoughts

Those mean judges reduced Penny Lancaster-Stewart to tears after her jive left them feeling less than impressed. 'Gangly, lumpy, laboured, very disappointing,' said Craig. 'This is not your dance.' Arlene added she had 'lazy legs,' and poor Penny ended up in the dance off. However, the judges decided to give snooker player Willie Thorne his cue to leave instead.

9. Anton Loses His Grin

After another bad week with partner Kate Garraway, Anton had a sense-of-humour failure. The couple's terrible tango was called 'distant and vacant', by Bruno: 'It was like you were not dancing with him.' A score of 15 left Anton fuming. 'They didn't give you the credit you deserve,' he roared. And calling the judges' comments 'nonsense', he stormed off down the corridor.

10. Matt and Flavia Kiss and Make Up

Matt and Flavia had become close during training but the week-four American jive was nearly the end of a beautiful relationship. Convinced Matt wasn't trying hard enough, Flavia stormed out. Matt made amends when he came back to the training room bearing gifts. 'Most girls after a row would expect an expensive gift,' he grinned. 'Flavia's happy with a chocolate muffin and a latte, and I love her for it.' Even so, he had sent her ten red roses the week before! The dance was a triumph, prompting Arlene to exclaim, 'Matt, can I call you Matinee Idol! That was a sensational smooth.'

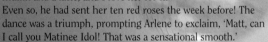

11. Dom-in-Aches

During training, cheeky chappy Dominic Littlewood decided to demonstrate the benefits of a crash mat to partner Lilia Kopylova – and promptly injured his shoulders. Sympathetic Lilia, of course, laughed her head off! Dom still managed to lift her on to his shoulders in the smooth and, in typical fashion, started and ended the dance with his hands on her rear. 'The bum thing was good because it tells a little story,' Craig commented. 'But it also stops you dancing a little bit, which is good.'

12. Logan's Run is Over

Bad boy Brendan was up to his old tricks and enraging the judges by putting an illegal lift into his American smooth with Kelly Brook. While Bruno raved Craig lamented, 'Brendan, why do you always go and ruin things? You put three lifts in and there are only two. It could have been a ten, and now we have to mark it down. That's stupidity.' Ever the rebel, Bruno gave them a ten anyway. There was more controversy when Gabby and Penny found themselves in the dance off – despite scores of 30 and 32. Len fumed, 'My role was to vote off one of the worst dancers, not one of the best!' A devastated Gabby was out.

John and Nicole

Letitia and Darren

Kenny and Ola

Penny and Ian

Matt and Flavia

Stephanie and Vincent

Willie and Erin

13. Kelly Brook No Argument

After apologizing for last week's illegal lifts, Brendan promised there would be 'no more shenanigans' but he wasn't banking on the stubborn nature of his partner! Kelly insisted that their paso doble should include a role reversal, and she became *Strictly*'s first female matador. The judges were not impressed. 'Instead of mucking about with this cape stuff, concentrate on the dance,' fumed Len. 'If you're back next week, come and do a proper dance, not all this ludicrous stuff.' Meanwhile, Kenny's kilted paso brought another first but landed the rugby player at the bottom of the board.

14. Everything Stops for Tea

Singer Alesha struggled with the genteel tradition of the foxtrot but help was at hand in the shape of her two devoted grandmothers. To get her in the mood they got partner Matthew to dress in 1940s army uniform and threw a tea dance. Their efforts worked and their beautiful dance had Bruno exclaiming, 'Heavenly elegance!' and Craig declaring the dance, 'Absolutely gorgeous.' Four nines put the couple at the top of the leader board.

15. Muma Mia!

Penny got a welcome surprise as she trained when her toddler son Alastair paid her a visit, wearing a sign reading 'Good Luck Muma'. And the foxtrot turned out to be her dance, with Craig commenting, 'You're certainly giving Alesha a run for her money. A triumph!' and Arlene raving, 'It's raining Pennys from heaven.' A score of 35 put her at number two. Letitia and Gethin both impressed the judges and landed 31, but it was a dance-off disaster for Dom when John Barnes managed to gain the judges' vote.

16. Kiss Me, Kate

After a relatively good score of 26 in week five, Kate struggled with the sexy salsa and even husband Derek Draper couldn't help. 'Obviously I find Kate phenomenally sexy,' he said. 'But she's not a showy sexy girl, she's more girl next door.' The resulting dance was more soggy than sultry and had  Bruno pronouncing, 'The nightmare is back!' But Len earned himself a smacker when he commented that it was 'A good effort. You're out of your comfort zone but you came out and performed and I congratulate you!'

17. The Boys are Back in Town

Just when the girls were leading the field, dark horses John Barnes and Gethin Jones crept up the inside to take pole position. After a few lessons with his son and salsa fan Jordan, John had Arlene, 'bathing in the ocean of that Cuban motion'. Gethin's Viennese waltz also had her in a lather, 'Tonight you were Gethin the gallant,' she said. 'Romantic, strong. Camilla, you were melting in his arms like whipped cream in a coffee.' Kelly and Brendan were also back on form with their own Viennese and all three couples scored 36.

18. Craig's Penny Whistle

Pretty Penny finally met her match in the mighty salsa, which Arlene dubbed 'A salsa from Stansted'. Craig that he was, 'not a fan, sadly'. Nonetheless, the judges were not happy when Penny and Ian found themselves in a dance off against Matt and Flavia. 'I think it's absolutely criminal these two couples are in the bottom two,' commented Craig and when Penny left, in floods of tears, the judges gave her a standing ovation and Craig demonstrated his Penny whistle. A clearly upset Matt lived to fight another day.

19. Letitia Gets Foxy

After partner Darren Bennett took Letitia Dean for an afternoon with a veteran foxtrot club, the *EastEnder* became the ballroom queen.

'To the ballroom reborn,' exclaimed Bruno and even Craig was impressed. 'Sweet, very stylish routine,' he said. 'Your shoulders were finally down.' Kelly and Brendan also wowed the judges with a sparkling jive, which Arlene called 'the closest I've seen to the legendary Jill Halfpenny and Darren jive'.

20. Camilla Gives Gethin the Eye

In an effort to bring out his romantic side, Camilla Dallerup treated Gethin to a romantic date on the London Eye, where they sipped champagne before dining on a boat on the Thames. Although they managed to scrape 31 points for the resulting rumba, not all the judges were impressed, with Len saying that 'all the romance is coming from Camilla,' and Craig claiming that 'something was missing'. Matt Di Angelo recovered well after stumbling in the quickstep, still earning a respectable 34.

21. A Painful Paso

Injured Kate had to have her back strapped up for her paso doble and was given sound advice by the physio. 'He came out with the classic line, "You'll be absolutely fine as long as you don't lift you arms or turn". Brilliant!' The dance didn't impress, with Arlene calling Kate 'less of a cape, more like a shag carpet'. She scored just 21 and, at last, the public agreed and Miss Garraway got away. At the other end of the scale Alesha's waltz gave Craig 'goosebumps'and had Bruno 'swept away in a sea of love'. The singer was elated to be awarded the first two tens of the series.

22. Nobody Puts Kenny in the Corner

To celebrate the twentieth anniversary of *Dirty Dancing*, a special group dance was choreographed by Kevin Marcel for the eighth show. The lads were all keen to perform the famous *Dirty Dancing* lift but burly Scotsman Kenny Logan was the obvious choice. Before the group dance, however, he went a step further, performing the show's first-ever one-armed lift in his American smooth. Show off!

23. Ear, Ear Brendan!

Brendan threw partner Kelly a samba party for her birthday and showed his appreciation of her dancing skills in training – by sticking his tongue in her ear! Sadly, the couple didn't have the dance licked and the judges mauled Brendan for his choreography. 'It's like hiring Judi Dench and then reading the Yellow Pages,' moaned Bruno. A tearful Kelly had to agree, telling her partner, 'Even I thought it was shocking!' Sadly, it was to be the couple's last dance as Kelly withdrew from the show due to a family tragedy.

24. John's Samba Swan-song

After surviving last week's dance off, a confident John Barnes claimed he was going to 'Samba my butt off!' But the judges were not impressed. 'Instead of being a riot, it was a murmur,' said Bruno, and Arlene accused him of 'having a love affair with the floor'. After coming up against rugby player Kenny in the dance off, the footballer got the boot. Matt Di Angelo gained his first two tens for a sexy salsa that had a flushed Arlene declaring, 'The Ramps returns!' But he was soon topped by Alesha's three tens for a cha-cha-cha, which Craig called 'fab – u – lous!'

25. Bruno's Dance Class

Matt's rumba with Flavia accomplished an unusual feat – it had all four judges in agreement about his lack of hip action. Ever the showman, Bruno yelled, 'Lubricate your hips,' before leaping up to show the *EastEnders* star exactly how it should be done. Len

hid his eyes in shame and Arlene joked, 'That wasn't romantic hips – that was gratuitous!'

26. Gethin Gets It

After frequent comments about Gethin's lack of personality on the dance floor, Camilla hired an acting coach who told him 'be Gethin, the Superhero'. The result was a dramatic turn-about. His waltz left Arlene swooning and Bruno crowning him the 'King of Romance', gaining him three tens and a score of 39. His shimmering salsa had Bruno recrowning him as 'the Loin King' and Len declaring, 'That acting coach was a miracle worker.' With a score of 74, the *Blue Peter* presenter shared the top spot with Alesha, whose ballroom dance had Arlene declaring, 'The tantalizing tango temptress triumphs!'

27. Soap Star Sickstep

After gaining the title of 'most improved dancer' from Bruno for last week's Viennese waltz, Letitia was distinctly off colour for her first double dance. With a nasty bug going around, the actress had to make a quick exit after her quickstep, to be sick in the toilet. After a so-so cha-cha-cha, a tearful Letitia found herself in the dance off with Kenny Logan. But the soap queen survived while the rugby player was finally kicked into touch.

28. Matt's Black Day

Feeling the pressure of his promise to Flavia that he would get her to the final, Matt Di Angelo succumbed to his nerves in the quarter-final foxtrot, giving up halfway through and sitting down on the steps. Sadly, the samba wasn't much better as, once again, he forgot his steps. The tearful lad then begged the audience to let him stay, saying, 'Maybe we can be excused for tonight and get past it for next week.' The viewers obliged and Matt was through.

29. Hot, Hot, Hot

Gethin's American smooth in the quarter-final had the judges arguing about what Arlene called 'horrible hands'. Craig agreed, while Len and Bruno decided his performance warranted perfect tens. The presenter followed that up with a jive that was so hot his trousers actually melted! 'I'm very excited! I absolutely loved that routine,' said Craig, and Gethin and Camilla found themselves at the top of the table with 75 out of 80.

30. Shock Dance Off

Alesha and Matt's Viennese waltz was so impressive that Len declared, 'If you don't get four tens, I'm going to go home and pickle my walnuts!' After receiving two nines and two tens, Matt Cutler joked, 'Shame about Len's walnuts.' An impressive paso doble left Alesha second on the board with a score of 74. But with Gethin on top, and Matt gaining the sympathy vote, the public vote left her in her first dance

off with Letitia. Not surprisingly, the first three judges chose to keep Alesha on for the semi-final. 'I did agree that it should be Alesha and Matt,' said Len, prompting Letitia to reply, 'I did too!'

31. Girl Power

Going into the semi-final as the last girl standing, Alesha asked, 'For the last two years of *SCD* a guy has won. Isn't it about time the girls got back on top?' And she soon showed the boys she meant business, with a 'neat and nippy' quickstep that had Arlene cooing in admiration, 'You are about to turn this semi-final into a killer competition.' The singer beamed as Bruno named her the 'first lady of dance' and she followed it up with an Argentine tango that earned her two more tens, bringing a total of 14 so far.

32. The Heart-throb Returns

After his disastrous quarter-final performance, Matt was determined not to let Flavia down again. 'Thinking about making a mistake or going blank is going through my head all the time so I need to learn it inside out,' he said. 'There are only two places in the final so I hope my nerves don't ruin it for me.' His elegant quickstep earned a respectable 35 but his real triumph was a winning waltz that brought Len to his feet. 'I'm going to do something I've never done before,' he said, as he gave the *EastEnder* a standing ovation. 'Winners never quit and quitters never win.' Bruno called the dance 'the biggest comeback since Judy Garland', and Matt and Flavia received the only perfect score of series five.

33. Gethin Gets Out

Gethin Jones was feeling the pressure at the beginning of the semi-final. 'It's got to be out of this world,' he said. 'It's got to be perfection.' In a clever bit of wardrobe design Camilla's skirt became his cape in the paso doble and the smouldering Welshman adopted a dominant stance that left his partner in agony with a shoulder injury and caused a row amongst the judges. Arlene said it was 'sometimes a Spanish omelette and sometimes a fine Rioja', prompting Len to quip, 'I've long been of the opinion I'm stuck here in the home for the bewildered!' before giving it a ten. Sadly it couldn't save the Welsh dragon from the dance off and the fire was put out.

34. You Lift Me Up

After the triumph of his perfect score Matt Di Angelo went into the final with everything to play for, in spite of the absence of his mum, who found his dancing too emotional to watch! Matt's sizzling salsa had Bruno raving, 'This salsa shakes those winter blues away,' and his American smooth earned a massive 39 points. 'You're up against one of the best girl celebrities we've ever had,' said Len. 'And yet, for me, you're matching your own, dance for dance.' As a final bid for the public vote the sexy soap star donned a skimpy vest and performed an impressive one armed lift in his freestyle dance. 'Completely fearless, and powerful,' said Craig. 'Loved it.'

35. Anything You Can Do ...

As Alesha wowed the judges with a wonderful waltz, a cheeky cha-cha-cha and a jubilant jive, the heat in the studio began to rise. 'Alesha, you're born to perform. Every dance is an absolute knockout,' beamed Len. 'This has got to be the closest fought final ever,' said a breathless Bruno. 'You two are the best of British and what young people should be all about. I am lost for words, for once.' As the couples faced the public vote Alesha was leading with 112 points but Matt was snapping at her heels with 110. Nail-biting stuff!

36. Viva la Diva!

After 112 dances, 12 weeks and 2800 hours of training the moment of truth arrived. 'I believe you are both running on a parallel at the moment and that's extraordinary because we've never had that,' commented Craig, before the result was announced. The audience and viewers were on the edge of their seats as Alesha was finally crowned as *Strictly*'s series-five queen. Emotions ran high as her family rushed on to the stage, Alesha cried tears of joy and dance partner Matt told her, 'You are a sheer joy to be with.' And she had been a sheer joy to watch!

Christine Bleakley

The last time presenter Christine Bleakley got up to dance was a bruising experience. She was in her boyfriend's pub in Belfast and when she went to work on *The One Show* the following Monday, she had such an enormous bruise on her leg the make-up artist had a job to cover it up.

In fact, *Strictly* will be putting the physios on stand-by because it seems Miss B is a little accident prone. She recently trained for the London Marathon but had to pull out when she broke her toe and she has a scar on her arm from when she was attacked by a flock of geese!

The 28-year-old presenter was born in Northern Ireland and started her television career behind the camera, training as a floor manager. 'I've done all the horrible jobs,' recalls Christine. 'I've made the tea, I've run after people, I've been at their beck and call – and I appreciate what the sound man has to do, I appreciate what the runner has to do to keep everybody happy, because I've gone through the ranks.'

Partner: Matthew Cutler

She became familiar to Irish viewers when she fronted *Skyhigh*, a programme that saw her flying around Ireland in a helicopter in 2004. Her big break in the UK came in 2007, when Myleene Klass unexpectedly went into labour, leaving *The One Show* without a presenter. Christine got a call, packed her bags and went straight to the airport, landing in London just in time for rehearsals: 'I might have looked calm but I was shaking with excitement and worried that I couldn't do it but desperate to get the chance.'

Christine is thrilled to be taking part in the show as she's a massive fan, so much so she even got audience tickets last year and took her best friend. 'It's a real honour to be part of *Strictly Come Dancing*,' she raves. 'So much so I have to keep pinching myself to make sure it's not a dream!'

Despite her high-profile job, Christine claims to be very shy and says she usually prefers other people being in the limelight. Her biggest challenge is going to be overcoming her nerves and letting her guard down in front of millions of TV viewers.

Although she has no dance experience, Christine says she is reasonably fit and, as her father was a professional musician, she is hoping that rhythm is in her blood!

Being partnered with last year's winning dancer, Matt Cutler, might bring added pressure but Christine is not eyeing the trophy just yet.

'I'm just going to concentrate on getting through each week,' she says. 'I'm not naïve enough to think there won't be any competitiveness but, not having done anything like this, my only concern at the moment is to perform to a standard that Matt is happy with. That will make me truly happy.'

Len's Low-down

The Most Impressive Dancer

Alesha Dixon was incredible, an absolutely fantastic dancer. I think she's probably the best that there's been and she was definitely the right winner.

The Worst Dancer

Kate Garraway was possibly the least talented but then again it could have been Willie Thorne. He did a surprisingly good ballroom dance but his tango wasn't much cop. Stephanie Beacham wasn't as good as I imagined she'd be but I don't think her heart was really in it.

Biggest Turn Round

Letitia Dean started off badly and didn't seem to overcome her nerves for weeks and weeks. Then, suddenly, she got it and her ballroom dancing was really good. Sometimes her Latin American wasn't of the same standard but they've got twelve dances to learn and, of course, you're going to feel more at home with some of them than others. It was the same with Gethin, who had that wonderful week when he went to the acting coach, who I called 'a miracle worker'. He went from having no attack and no personality on the floor suddenly to everything kicking in.

The Biggest Surprise

My biggest surprise was John Barnes when he did his salsa in week six. I gave it a ten because I thought it was fantastic and so unexpected. He'd been fairly average and then he suddenly came out and really worked it. He danced it perfectly and it suited him and his style of dancing. He has a stooping posture, which, for ballroom and most of the Latin dances, you don't want but it doesn't matter for the salsa, which is down and dirty. That dance was one of my highlights.

Best Dancers Over All Five Series

Jill Halfpenny was wonderful in Latin and her jive is still one of the best dances we've seen. Alesha was best in ballroom, very talented and extremely elegant. As an all-rounder, my favourite so far is Colin Jackson. It was only because Erin and he chose to use puppets in the freestyle dance that they lost – unfortunately it was an idea that just didn't work for them.

If you've managed to get to the final, you know you can get nines and tens. What I don't understand is why they spend weeks learning ballroom and Latin and then do a disco dance.

Worst Moment

The biggest memory for me of series five was the terrible situation when Gabby Logan and Penny Lancaster-Stewart were in the bottom two, which shouldn't have happened. Craig voted to keep Gabby, and the other two went for Penny so it was left to me to chuck one off and I had to choose Gabby. That's the thing that stands out in my memory.

The Worst Dancer Over All Five Series

It's still Quentin Willson for me. What is bizarre is you never really know who will be good until you are on the show.

The Winner's Story
From Pop Princess to Dance Diva

Stunning Alesha Dixon credited *Strictly* for turning her life around after her series-five triumph. Twelve months before getting her hands on the glittering trophy the singer was at 'a real, real low point' having gone through a very public split from husband MC Harvey and been dropped by her record company.

'I thought 2007 was going to be terrible, but because of *Strictly* my confidence is back,' she said, after beating Matt Di Angelo in one of the closest finals to date. 'Dancing saved me. I've got the real me back. This is the best Christmas present ever.'

As a child, Alesha had started tap lessons but had to drop out because her family couldn't afford to carry on with them, so the former Mis-Teeq singer didn't have to be asked twice to take the *Strictly* challenge.

'I've always wondered how far I could have gone with it if I could have carried on and how far I could have pushed myself,' she said, when she agreed to take part in the show.

During Alesha's career in the successful R 'n' B band she'd had a number of dance routines to perform but, initially, Alesha didn't think that would help her on the show. 'They were street dances, which are completely different,' she says. 'So the thing I'm most worried about is not living up to my partner's expectations.' She needn't have worried, from day one she hardly put a foot wrong and at one point partner Matt Cutler said, 'She's very precious to me and I wish I could keep her.'

She impressed the judges before she'd even performed a competitive dance. After the ladies' group dance in the first show Bruno predicted her success. 'The men should be afraid, very afraid, because these girls mean business,' he said. 'How to pick a jewel from all these wonderful girls? But I would say, the two hot brunettes – Alesha and Kelly.'

Her first dance, a rumba, which put her in third place with 31, had Len declaring, 'You're a contender,' and her second competitive dance, a jive, earned her an amazing 36. 'Another

fantastic routine,' said Craig. 'The sheer energy was amazing and your finishes are perfect.'

Devoted grandmothers Clem and Maureen, who were on hand every week to offer support and encouragement, were over the moon. 'I knew when I got the nines my family would be bouncing off the walls,' she said the following week.

From there, Alesha went from strength to strength, racking up nines for every routine and staying consistently in the top two couples. Her week-seven waltz raised the bar with her first perfect tens from Arlene and Bruno, with the latter declaring, 'I'm in love – I think everyone is!' Even harsh judge Craig admitted: 'That actually gave me goosebumps!'

The following week her feat was matched by Matt Di Angelo, only for Alesha to go one better and land herself three tens and a score of 39 for her cha-cha-cha.

'I was the king of dance,' complained her disgruntled opponent. 'Alesha has blown us out of the water!'

By the end of the quarter-finals Alesha had already scored more tens than any contestant in history, with a grand total of ten. Despite her high scores, the quarter-finals saw Alesha tackle her first dance off, as the public voted to keep a wobbly Matt Di Angelo. The judges were faced with a choice between Letitia Dean and Darren Bennett or Alesha and Matt Cutler. They were unanimous, with Arlene saying, 'I never want to stop watching her dance,' and Craig calling the couple 'near perfect'.

The final saw her pitted against the dashing young Matt Di Angelo, who proved a worthy opponent. 'Matt, you've proved to everyone you deserve to be in the final tonight,' Len told him. 'Alesha, you've been Miss Consistency throughout. It doesn't matter what dance is thrown at you, you come out with elegance and poise. You're the complete package.'

After five spectacular dances, culminating in the freestyle dance to 'I Need a Hero', Alesha took the crown.

'I need a hero,' raved Arlene. 'Tonight, Alesha, you are my heroine.'

Craig added, 'You dance as if your life depended on it. Fantastic.'

Twelve months on from one of the lowest points in her life, singer Alesha Dixon was reborn as a dancing superstar, and she couldn't have been happier. 'I've learnt to dance,' she beamed. 'I'm happy and I believe it was meant to happen. *Strictly* has just given me a real zest for life. I thrive on hard work and even though my body is in pain and tired, my first choice is to get up and do something. Life is so short. We should all grasp it.'

The judges on Alesha

'She does class and she does sexy. She does beauty and she does beast. What more do you want?'
Bruno

'You're born to perform. Every dance is an absolute knock-out.'
Len

'You are the real deal. You glimmer, you shimmer, you shine and you bring warmth to everything you do.'
Arlene

'She is full of sass and she's hot, hot, hot.'
Craig

'My pulse is racing. My heart is pounding. It's diva time!'
Bruno

'I could watch you all night, I really could. Absolutely sensational.'
Craig

Tom Chambers

Tom Chambers has his dancing feet to thank for his role as *Holby City*'s dashing doctor Sam Strachan. Three years ago, Tom made a short film in which he performed a famous dance from Fred Astaire's 1937 movie, *A Damsel in Distress.* He taught himself Astaire's complex steps and spent months on the project, filmed at his old primary school in Derbyshire, before sending it to hundreds of producers, directors and casting directors around the country.

The totally brilliant routine caught the eye of *Holby City's* casting director Julie Harkin who was looking for a new doctor for the show and invited Tom to audition. Tom joined the cast on 3 January 2006 and was an instant hit with the female audience.

The routine also proved a huge hit with YouTube viewers and received unanimous praise on the message boards. Tom is now hoping to replicate this popularity with his Saturday-night dances and hopes the show might lead to him fulfilling his ultimate ambition: to make and appear in a *Singin' in the Rain*-style British movie.

In the past, the *Holby* heart-throb has shown a determination to dance that will serve him well in the competition. At drama school, aged 19, he was unable to convince any of his classmates to be his dance partner in a choreography competition so he borrowed a mannequin from a local clothes shop to dance with instead. 'I performed a routine where I swung the mannequin between my legs and around my back,' he recalls. 'We ended up winning first prize in the competition.' After the unforgettable Colin Jackson dummy dance, the judges will be hoping he doesn't try and revive that routine for the show!

Tom is a huge fan of tap dancing and is hoping to incorporate it into one of the routines.

'I'm looking forward to the ballroom most,' he says, 'because I can't wait to wear the posh costumes. One of my favourite songs is Cole Porter's "Night and Day" and I'd like to dance to it at some point. Listening to that song is like floating on a cloud to me.'

If anyone has cause to doubt his dedication to the *Strictly* journey, it's not his immensely understanding fiancée, TV researcher Claire. The couple were due to wed on Saturday 18 October, but had to move the wedding to the following day because of the show. And, just in case he is still competing after that, he's even cancelled his honeymoon!

Partner: *Camilla Dallerup*

The Latin Dances

A good dance routine is like a garden. If the lawn is the basic dance, then you want to see a beautiful flower here and a beautiful flower there. All lawn is too bland, as is a dance that is all basic steps, but equally, all flowers becomes a riot of colour and movement and visually one flower fights against the other. You need the grass to complement the beauty of the flowers. That's true of all the dances on *Strictly* – a beautiful mix of lawn and flowers!

The rumba

The rumba is a dance of romance so there should be romantic interplay between the couple. Latin dancing is about a divorce between your upper and lower body. From your waist down your body is the rhythm while your upper body is the melody. To get the correct lower body you have to get the correct feet, which in turn works your legs, which in turn works your hips, so it's not about wiggling your bum.

Hip movement comes from the leg. If you're waiting for a bus you would have one leg straight and the hip out. When you get fed up with that you straighten the other leg and the other hip goes out, so it's the straightening of the legs that should cause the hips to work.

When you've mastered that you have to get the upper body to show the musicality, so that is quite a difficult thing to do.

What the judges look for:

- A nice mixture of steps so it's not all tricks. They want to see some basic steps and the fundamentals of the dance, as well as some clever choreography
- A nice hip action
- Romance and interplay

Best Couple: Natasha Kaplinsky and Brendan Cole performed a beautiful rumba in series one, for a score of 36.

Worst Couple: Fiona Phillips and Brendan Cole had their rumba branded a 'complete dance disaster' in series three, and scored 13 points.

The samba

The samba is a party dance, a carnival dance, and that's how it should come across. It's the most difficult of all the Latin dances because most of the dances have got the same rhythm throughout but, in the samba, you have all different rhythms. You have quick-quick-slow, you've got slow-quick-quick, you've got one and two and so on. The dance also moves around the floor. The rumba, the cha-cha-cha and the jive are what we call stationary dances – although they move a little bit they don't actually travel around the room. The samba does. So in addition to all the different rhythms, you've got steps that are on the spot and you've got steps that will travel. On top of that, you have to show a devil-may-care carnival expression.

What the judges look for:
- Good hip action
- Good rhythm
- Fast feet
- Steps that are placed and steps that travel
- A taste of the Mardi Gras

Best Couple: Zoe and Ian
Bruno called Zoe Ball 'the samba Queen' after her performance in week five of series three and the same dance landed her and partner Ian Waite 38 points in the final.

Worst Couple: Christopher Parker and Hanna Karttunen scored just 15 with their series-one samba.

The Latin Dances

The cha-cha-cha

They call it the cheeky cha-cha-cha because it should be a little bit cheeky. It's a fun, flirty dance and you want to see a little bit of interplay. There are a few different stories about how the cha-cha-cha and the rumba developed years ago, but they come from Cuba and the story goes that when the slaves had been working on the sugar plantations, they took all the wood and foliage that they'd chopped down and made a bonfire at the end of the day. While the fire was burning they'd get out a few bongos and have a dance in a similar way to the cha-cha-cha: fun and a little bit sexy. As the evening drew on, and the embers died down to a warm glow, then the music would slow up and they'd start dancing more of a rumba. It's a bit like when you're a teenager and you go to a party – you dance fast at the beginning but, at the end of the night, you're all snogging on the sofa to the slow numbers!

So the cha-cha-cha is the fun version of the romantic rumba, because they're very similar steps, except that the cha-cha-cha has one more step in the basic.

What the judges look for:

- Good hip action
- Fun and flirting
- Strong arms and good finishes at the fingers
- Toes turned out and strong lines

Best Couple: Alesha Dixon and Matthew Cutler scored 39 in week eight of series five and 38 for the same dance in the final.

Worst Couple: Quentin Willson's series-two cha-cha-cha scored a pathetic 8 points and led Craig to dub him, 'Britain's Worst Dancer'.

The salsa

The salsa is a very popular dance, a club dance, and a mixture of a number of other dance styles. Salsa means sauce, hot and spicy, and it's a blend of elements from mambo, samba and cha-cha-cha. It's not one of the ten dances usually performed at competitions, so even the professionals sometimes struggle and some of them seek help – Flavia and Matt had choreographer and teacher Richard Marcel come in to help them on the last series and others have done the same.

What the judges look for:

- As in all the Latin dances (with the exception of the paso doble) they can be summed up with three words: rhythm, rhythm, rhythm
- Like a salsa dip it should be hot and spicy
- Sexy hip movements
- Legs that are fast and loose

Best Couple: Who could forget the sizzling salsa from **Mark Ramprakash and Karen Hardy** in series four? It earned top marks and, as Arlene said, it was 'Hot, hot, hot!'

Worst Couple: **Kate Garraway and Anton du Beke** scored 18 and had Bruno declaring; 'The nightmare is back!'

Jodie Kidd

At 6 foot 1 inch, Jodie Kidd is the tallest female celebrity taking part in this series, and believes her height may be a hindrance in the Latin dances. 'Being tall and riding horses all my life, correct posture has always been something that has been drummed into me,' says the leggy blonde. 'Growing up I was a bit of a stooper and was embarrassed by my height so I was always bending down to fit in with my smaller friends. My mother taught me to be proud of my height and always sit and stand with straight posture, which might help in ballroom dance.

Partner: Ian Waite

'The Latin might be more difficult for me because I'm all legs and arms. It's very fast, and I may struggle with the quick flicks and turns that smaller, more compact people can do.'

What she lacks in technique, Jodie is bound to make up for in enthusiasm, if past form is anything to go by. A complete novice when challenged by *Top Gear* to try and achieve the fastest lap in a racing car, she beat such petrol heads as Jay Kay and Jeremy Clarkson and held the record for quite some time. She also threw herself into a new racing career and, in 2004, was chosen to join the Maserati racing team where she was nicknamed 'Queen of the Rain' for her ability to drive very quickly in bad weather. She has also taken part in several Gumball 3000 rallies, an annual 3000-mile round the world event that takes place on public roads.

Jodie, who has been modelling since she was discovered on a Barbados beach at 15, is also passionate about horses and is a keen polo player. The game has often taken her to Argentina, where she once attended an Argentine tango show and fell in love with the dance. 'It was completely mesmerizing and something I really wanted to learn myself,' she says. While work commitments meant she never got round to joining a class, she is delighted to be given the opportunity now.

Jodie loves a new challenge and is a keen participant in extreme sports, and she also admits to being exceptionally competitive. When it comes to *Strictly* the difference for her is that she is not in total control. 'If I'm in a racing car or on a horse, then how well I do is up to me and how far I push myself, whether it's braking late at a bend in motor racing or really pushing for a ride off in polo.

'But in this show it's also down to the audience who are voting at home and if they don't like you then you are leaving the show.'

Global Glitz

The glamour and glitz of *Strictly Come Dancing* has now had a global impact, showing in more than 30 countries, under various different names. The title of the Chinese version translates roughly as 'Miracle Dancing', in Germany it's called *Let's Dance* and in Finland, *Dances with Stars* – intended as a pun on the film *Dances with Wolves*. In Norway, the title is *Skal vi danse?* Or *Shall we dance?*

After its success in the UK, Australia was the first to take on the show, as *Dancing with the Stars*, and judges include Paul Mercurio, the star of *Strictly Ballroom,* and theatre performer Todd McKenney.

The format soon appeared in countries around the world, including Brazil, Chile, Panama, Norway, India, Slovakia and Russia. The US began screening *Dancing with the Stars* in 2005, with our very own Len Goodman and Bruno Tonioli on the panel, and Craig Revel Horwood was soon drafted in to add his unique brand of criticism to the New Zealand version.

In 2006, the format became the world's most popular television programme, reaching the top-ten shows in 17 countries. In fact, Australia and the United States love it so much that they do it twice a year!

Last year's Australian trophy went to *McLeod's Daughter* actress, Bridie Carter, who gained two perfect scores in the final for her samba and foxtrot. The spring season saw the lovely Kimberley Davies, former *Neighbours* star, eliminated in the second show while *Home and Away* actor Tim Campbell made it all the way to the semi-finals. Singer Kate Ceberano lifted the glitterball in the closely fought final.

In New Zealand the 2008 title was won by netball player Temepara George, partnered by Stefano Olivieri.

The US *Dancing with the Stars* saw more than its fair share of Hollywood glamour with Jane Seymour, Priscilla Presley, Steve Guttenberg and Oscar-winning actress Marlee Matlin taking to the floor. Other big names included Marie Osmond, Monica Seles, American footballer Jason Taylor, boxer Floyd Mayweather and our very own Mel B.

'In the United States the pool is bigger than the UK and the industry is bigger,' says Bruno. 'The show has a rising momentum so it's easy for them to get movie stars. As well as our Oscar winner we had a Tony winner, Marissa Jaret Winokur.

'Even the sports stars are huge. Jason Taylor is like David Beckham in America. And they're less self-conscious about taking part. The Brits are always a little more reserved.'

Bruno admits that he doesn't always know who the US stars are but that's not a problem.

'I don't know who the hell they are,' he laughs. 'I'm backwards and forwards so much I don't see much TV. Len and I are both the same, we are always saying, "Who the heck is that?" Regardless of who they are, I don't let it affect me. As a judge you call it as you see it. You can't let somebody's standing, or fame, affect your judgement. We couldn't care less, to be honest!'

Verdict: Len and Bruno

Mel B

The Spice Girl proved a fantastic contestant throughout the competition and even got the highest judges' scores in the final of season five, with a score of 85 out of 90. The public, however, chose Indy driver Hélio Castroneves (pictured right) as their champion.

Bruno: Mel B really surprised me – she was brilliant. Her paso doble was one dance I will never forget. She did a paso doble dominatrix style, which was amazing. She had an amazing outfit all made from black leather and the look of it, the choreography and the way she danced, was unique. She came second in the competition, although she came first with the judges. Mel is really good fun, incredibly hard-working because she was preparing for the Spice Girls tour at the time and everyone loved her. She really is a nice, regular girl and her dancing was a revelation.

Len: Mel B was fabulous and she really should have won. She was the judges' winner but, in the final, the viewers went for Hélio. Mel's paso doble was probably the best paso I've ever seen. It was bloody brilliant.

Global Glitz

Marie Osmond

The singer and mother of eight did remarkably well in season five, making it to the final and coming third. But she had one very wobbly moment …

Len: Marie did the samba and then came over, like they do in the UK show, to hear the judges' comments. I was asked what we look for in a samba and I said, 'The samba is a very rhythmic dance and you want to see lots of hip action–' And, suddenly, down she went. Shock-horror! She was out cold!

Fortunately, it was in America because the host, Tom Bergeron, was able to say, 'Let's go to a commercial break.' So they cut to the adverts and while they were on they got her up and off the stage. When she came back she told us that when she's doing something very intense she forgets to breathe. Evidently, she held her breath throughout the 90-second samba.

She recovered nicely and no doubt got millions of votes from people who felt sorry for her, so she carried on for the next two or three weeks.

Marie got right through to the last three, which is surprising when she's a woman in her late forties with eight kids. I told Marie there was no point in trying to compete against the others if they can do back flips. Go with your strengths. She had been in show business since she was three years old and was a great performer.

Bruno: Marie was a good dancer but in the last dance, the freestyle, she went a bit barmy. I called her 'The Bride of Chucky meets Baby Jane' because it was so insane. It was on a par with the real classic, the one that Erin Boag and Colin Jackson did, with the inflatable dummies. That's when they lose the plot on the last dance and basically make fools of themselves, but it's good fun.

Monica Seles

The Serbian-born player has numerous Grand Slam titles under her belt, but it seems she was foxed by the foxtrot. She was eliminated after two weeks in season six, scoring a meagre 15 on both occasions.

Len: I imagined Monica Seles was going be good because, for tennis, you've got to have coordination – which is one of the keys for dancing – you've got to have timing and rhythm and you've got to be fit. But she had absolutely no coordination when it came to dancing. She was awful, which surprised everybody.

Bruno: Poor Monica was terrible! Such a nice girl but she really was even worse than Kate Garraway. She couldn't even take the mickey out of herself, she was so petrified.

Jane Seymour

The British actress and former Bond girl was eliminated on week seven of season five, after a disappointing cha-cha-cha.

Bruno: Jane was great. She was brilliant at ballroom; she has such beautiful posture. Latin was not something that came naturally to her but she did incredibly well. What a beautiful lady.

Len: Jane Seymour was the most elegant lady you could ever wish to see. She'd obviously been ballet trained as a child and her ballroom dancing was beautiful. She had elegance, she had poise and she had the most musical arms. Her Latin American wasn't quite so good but it's hard for a 56 year old to be raunchy. Latin is more of a young person's dance whereas ballroom needs elegance. Jane had a lovely figure and great musicality so that was perfect for her.

Priscilla Presley

The wife of the King didn't manage to become a ballroom queen, in season six. In fact she was banished from the court after scoring 21 for their week-five rumba.

Len: I only spoke to Priscilla once and she wasn't very warm but maybe I caught her on a bad day. Maybe she was nervous. But I admire her pluck. She was over 60 and did some lovely ballroom dancing. She wasn't much good at the Latin but that tends to suit younger dancers.

Bruno: Priscilla did very well. It's tough because the girls were so good this year. Kristi Yamaguchi, who won, never got less than nine. It was incredible and the choreography was amazing.

Steve Guttenberg

The star of *Police Academy* found himself marched off set after his foxtrot failed to save his bacon in season six.

Bruno: He wasn't very good, bless him! But a nice guy. Very funny.

Len: I've never met anyone who was so in love with *Dancing with the Stars*. He loved it and he thought it was the most marvellous show. He was totally enthusiastic and thought everyone should do it.

Darren Bennett

Brendan Cole

Like James and Ola Jordan, **Darren** and dance partner Lilia Kopylova are husband and wife, having married in 1999. They are also the only dance partnership to have won a series of *Strictly Come Dancing* each – Darren scooping series two with Jill Halfpenny, and Lilia powering to victory a year later with Darren Gough.

Watching Lilia in series three, having been knocked out in the fourth week with Gloria Hunniford, was tough for Darren, but he was full of pride.

'Not being able to perform and showcase yourself as a dancer is very hard,' he admits. 'But if I can't win, I would love my wife to do it!'

Darren's parents are professional dancers who own a dance school in Sheffield, which is one of the largest in the country. He and twin brother Dale started training at the age of six.

'Dancing was something I've grown up with; it seems a natural progression that I'm involved in the sport,' he recalls. 'When I was about 20 I did question why I did it but realized that I did love it, rather than doing it just because I always have.'

Competing from the age of seven, Darren danced with the same partner for 14 years. When she decided to give it up, brother Dale introduced him to Russian dancer Lilia.

The couple, who both teach, reckon that their close relationship is mirrored in their routines. 'People see more of us now,' says Darren. 'Not just dancing, but also our personalities.'

Brendan was not an instant convert to dance when – aged six – his mum took him and his brother Scott to classes. In fact, he hated it so much he had to be dragged there kicking and screaming!

He may not have liked dance, but dance clearly liked him and he was competing by the time he was seven, going on to become the Juvenile, Junior and Youth Champion of New Zealand.

Along with his brother and sister, who danced as a partnership, the Cole family made a considerable impression on the New Zealand ballroom world but, at 18, Brendan decided that Latin American was more up his street.

Feeling he had risen as far as he could in New Zealand, he decided to come to Britain, where he could work with the best teachers and find a new partner. Being a perfectionist, it took him a year to find the right girl. In 1996, he met Camilla Dallerup, his partner on and off the dance floor for the next eight years.

Brendan's start on *Strictly Come Dancing* couldn't have been better. Partnered with the elegant Natasha Kaplinsky in series one, he went on to win the first trophy.

The next three series, partnering Fiona Phillips, Sarah Manners and Claire King, were more disappointing.

The last series saw Brendan coupled with his dream girl Kelly Brook. 'Last year our partnership was perfect,' he recalls. 'Kelly was fun and determined to do well.'

This year, Brendan is firing up for a challenging series, which he thinks will be, 'harder than ever, more competition and more pressure, tempers will fray and probably not just mine!'

Speciality: Latin American
Professional Achievements: UK Closed Professional Latin Champion; British National Professional Latin Champion; World Professional Latin Finalist; British Show Dance Champion; World Professional Rising Star Champion

---

Speciality: Latin American
Professional Achievements: Asia Pacific Latin American Champion; Four times New Zealand Latin American Champion; World Open Latin Dance Semi-Finalists; International Open Latin Dance Semi-Finalists; British Open Latin Dance Semi-Finalists

Matthew Cutler

Matthew joined *Strictly* in series three. Although he was knocked out of the competition first with actress Siobhan Hayes, he made up for it in series five when he was partnered with Alesha Dixon.

'Winning was like a dream come true for me. Alesha was amazing. The whole experience was mad, exciting, exhausting – I loved it!'

Essex boy Matthew started learning at eight after his mum, who competed in the 'Old Time' competitions, suggested he tried it. He was a natural.

'I used to ride to dance classes at the local church every Saturday and then go home and show my mum what I had learnt. The teachers were just teaching the steps and foot positions. So I used to practise at home and the next week I would show them my routine – it was all due to Mum, really.'

The teachers teamed him with a girl from the school to compete. Once again Matthew's mum helped out, sewing the costumes.

One of the judges suggested he and his new partner compete in an open contest and, at ten, he did just that. At 12, he found a new partner and at 14 they became England's No. 2 couple and were placed in all major competitions including British National Championships, Open British Championships (Blackpool) and International Championships. For the last year and a half of the Junior section, they were England's No. 1 couple and undefeated champions in all the major competitions.

Speciality: Latin American
Professional Achievements: World and European Professional Latin Finalist; UK Closed Professional Latin Champion; International Professional Latin Finalist; Closed British Professional Latin Champion; World, Open British, International and UK Open Professional Latin Finalist; World Masters Professional Latin Champion

Anton Du Beke

Series five was the most challenging yet for **Anton** and dance partner Erin Boag. Anton struggled with the lovely Kate 'two left feet' Garraway, while Erin and celebrity partner Willie Thorne only made it to week three.

The son of a Spanish mother and Hungarian father, Anton was born and raised in Sevenoaks. His early passion was football; however, he was lured into the world of dance at 14, when he went to pick his sister up from her ballroom lesson and discovered how many girls he could meet there!

Having trained in both Latin American and ballroom, Anton chose ballroom at 17 because he thinks Latin American dancing is 'a bit of a nonsense, but don't tell the others that! I always loved the tradition and class of the ballroom, which made sense to me.'

To fund his amateur career, Anton took a job as a baker, starting at 3 a.m., working a full day and then training in the afternoon. He and Erin have danced together for over ten years. When not on the show, Anton teaches in London.

The first series, when he came third with Lesley Garrett, was Anton's biggest *Strictly* success so far. Other partners have included Esther Rantzen, Jan Ravens and Patsy Palmer.

'Dancing with Patsy was great fun,' he says. 'It was exciting as well because of the unpredictability. She's a very sweet girl who speaks first and thinks of the consequences later.'

Anton doesn't mind who he is paired with as long as the celebrity knows the show well but, in his typically modest way, he explains that his worst fear is working with someone who 'doesn't think I'm the best dancer in the world!'

Speciality: Ballroom
Professional Achievements: IDTA Classic Champion; British National Finalist; BDF Star Ball Finalist; UK & International Rising Star Finalist; UBC Canadian Champion

Phil Daniels

Last year Flavia Cacace danced her way into the final with *EastEnder* Matt Di Angelo and this year she'll try to do the same thing with his dad! Phil Daniels played Matt's onscreen father, Kevin Wicks, in the BBC soap so he'll no doubt be asking runner-up Matt for a few tips.

Phil first leapt to fame in cult movie, *Quadrophenia*, where he played teenage mod Jimmy. He became a household name to a whole new generation when he provided the vocals for Blur's classic hit *Parklife* and became a familiar face to soap fans after joining *EastEnders* in 2006. Phil's character made a dramatic exit on New Year's Eve 2007 when he was killed in a horrific car crash.

Partner: *Flavia Cacace*

Phil first got the acting bug as a teenager when he encountered the improvisation-based training techniques of Anna Scher. 'She used to go around the local schools doing workshops,' he recalls. 'Me and a mate did it for a couple of days and took the mick really. But I quite liked it, so I got the address of her school in Islington and carried on going.'

Despite his stint at stage school, Phil never learnt to dance. He did star in the musical *Carousel* where, he claims, 'I was slung around a bit! I ran around a bit and jumped up and down but I wouldn't call it dancing.'

The last time Phil danced was in a bar on the beach in Spain when he was on holiday. 'It was probably "Viva Espana" or something awful like that and I was dragged on to the dance floor!' he remembers. 'But I'm a rubbish dancer and I reckon I have two left feet.'

The 49-year-old actor, who lives with partner Jan and their teenage daughter, is looking forward to learning a new skill and having some fun and he hopes he will surprise himself. His main worry is that he'll fall over live on air. While he enjoys watching the Latin, he thinks he is better suited to the waltz because there's more control.

At least the panel of judges, a terrifying prospect at the best of times, includes one familiar face. Arlene was the choreographer on the musical of *A Clockwork Orange,* in which he starred. 'I think we got on well,' he ponders. 'She didn't criticize me for anything!' Phil thinks he'll be able to take constructive criticism and believes Len is a fair judge, but he is a little bit wary of Craig's reputation and says he will defend himself if the comments are malicious or unfair.

Word of warning, Craig – Phil is a trained knife-thrower!

Strictly Sp

While nearly 13 million tune in to *Strictly Come Dancing* during its autumn run, only a handful of people get to watch it in the studio. In January 2008, fans up and down the country finally got the chance to experience the thrill of the live experience when the tour took to the road.

Nine celebrity dancers and their partners performed to audiences of over 10,000 in seven venues around the UK. During the 40 dates, fans thrilled to the sight of Zoe Ball's triumphant tango, sighed over Darren Gough's flirtatious foxtrot and laughed their head off over Chris Parker's perky paso doble.

'We wanted great dancers as well as some who were not so great, but were very amusing, like Chris Parker,' explains Paul Roberts of Phil McIntyre Enterprises, who helped stage the show.

'We didn't want it to be black and white, a "best of" *Strictly*. We wanted it to embrace the whole spirit of *Strictly Come Dancing*.

'Executive Producer Sam Donnelly and Arlene Phillips decided on the best dances for each celebrity and we always knew that Christopher Parker running around with a cape would be a crowd pleaser!'

Although the *Strictly* spectacular kicked off in January, planning started in the summer of 2007. But it wasn't until a week before the tour that all those involved came together to rehearse.

'Because the professional dancers, and of course Matt Di Angelo, were involved in the TV show right up to the end, we didn't get everyone together until a week before,' says Paul. 'It was all rehearsed but it had to come together very quickly. We couldn't start focusing on the live show until the TV show was finished. The execution of it came together very quickly, with a lot of help from Sam Donnelly, Arlene Phillips and the professional dancers who all worked very hard for that week.'

Before it all came together, however, there was the set and lighting to sort out. First on board was Patrick Doherty, the designer of the studio set, who came up with a bigger version for the huge arenas that the tour would visit.

Above all the set, the lighting and massive dance floor had to be portable, easily dismantled and very quick to put together again.

Production coordinator Andy Gibbs oversaw the preparations for the events. 'For a few of the shows we arrived at six in the morning and had a performance at

2 p.m., so we had to design the set so we could put it together quickly,' he explains.

'We made 900 square metres of dance floor, which breaks up into 1200 panels, and we had to be able to lay it in two hours. How much of the dance floor we put down depended on the size and shape of the venue. Generally we put 800 square metres (20 metres by 40 metres) down but in places like Glasgow, where the seating is very different, the venue is wider and not as deep, we did 30 metres by 30 metres – hence the 900 square metres.

'The set itself is big. We got 21 star cloths made, of red crimson, and they were each 6 metres wide and 11 metres deep. We had all sorts of screens, a lot of projection and a vast amount of lighting. On the TV show they have over 600 ChromaStrips, which are tubes of light that change colour. On the live show we ended up with 304 of those.

'All the music was played live so we also toured a 19-piece orchestra, as well as four singers. Then we needed two sound desks, two sound mixers, someone who deals with all the effects, the video sound and the radio mikes then a separate person who dealt with all the orchestra.

'We ended up in twelve 45-foot trucks, with two buses for the artists, and three buses for the crew. The caterers were feeding over 90 people on a daily basis.'

The costumes alone took up half a truck. That's a lot of sequins and a lot of laundry!

'A lot of the stuff had to be dry-cleaned and there are specialist dry-cleaners around the country who are used to doing that stuff. Because you're doing multiple dates in these places, not just one show and moving on, we often had the following morning to get things clean so a lot of washing and ironing gets done.'

Of course, not all of the costumes could be properly cleaned in time, so the costume department had to find other ways of keeping them fresh.

'I didn't go on the tour,' says costume designer Su Judd. 'But there's a whole team of clever girls who look after the dresses. The dancers wear the same dresses every night and as they come off, they get sprayed and dried and put in a hot box. Some of them were only cleaned once during the whole tour. In between, they are literally wiped down with baby wipes. You'd have thought they would get a bit smelly but actually they weren't that bad.

'I went to see the final show and the costumes held up really well. They are made specifically for dancing so they are 100 per cent lycra that doesn't show sweat patches and breathes very well. It's the fake tan that makes the worst smell, which is ghastly.'

Although they were all performing familiar routines the dancers had to rethink the area they covered for the purposes of the tour. With the floor almost four times bigger than the one in the BBC studio that meant a lot of legwork.

'We expanded the routines but we can only do it to a certain extent,' says professional dancer Ian Waite. 'Some of us haven't got that long legs and the floor is absolutely enormous, so it wouldn't be possible to cover it, unless we had a ten-minute routine. We only have a minute and a half so we get round it as well as we can.'

As all the celebrities come from different series, it was also impossible for every one of them to dance with their orginal partner, so one or two had to get used to dancing with a new professional.

'I was dancing with Zoe Ball for the tour,' explains Ian. 'But I danced with Denise Lewis in series two so she ended up dancing with Matthew Cutler for the live show.

'I've danced with Zoe more recently than Denise so it made sense, and it was great to dance with her again. At the same time it's lovely to have Denise around. We came second on the series and had so much fun together, so its like having a best mate around.

'I did help Denise and Matthew with the routine because they're doing the quickstep that we choreographed together, so that was great fun too.'

Strictly Spectacular

Most shows would ask you to turn your mobile phones off – but not *Strictly Come Dancing Live*. After all, it wouldn't be the same without an audience vote to put the wind up the judges!

Each couple danced one Latin routine and one ballroom, performing the same dances on each of the 40 dates. After watching the dances and listening to the judges' comments the audience were asked, as usual, to cast their votes via phone. The amazing thing was that, while the dances were the same, there was a different winner each night.

'Everybody danced differently every night,' says Ian Waite. 'Some people danced brilliantly one night and then had an off night, while others improved over the course of the tour. That's why the marks varied and that's good because it would be very boring if you got the same marks and the same comments.

'It kept us on our toes because nobody can win every night, and we still had to put in a performance. No one wants to put in a mediocre performance in front of 10,000 people.'

Although Bruno Tonioli couldn't make the tour, Len, Arlene and Craig sat in judgement each night while a heavily pregnant Kate Thornton took on the role of both Tess and Bruce to become the sole host.

Unlike the TV show, of course, the judges had to come up with a different comment for the same dance – 40 times over. As a result, Craig reveals, they were often hoping for a slip-up.

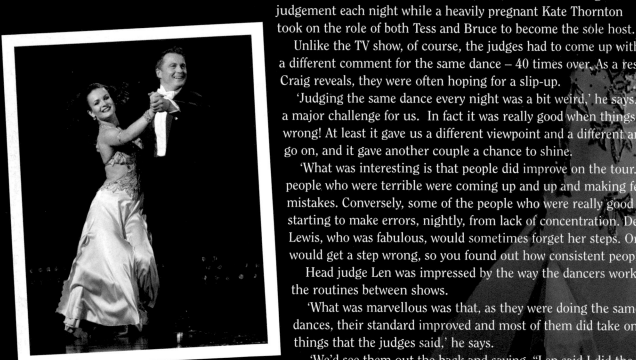

'Judging the same dance every night was a bit weird,' he says. 'It was a major challenge for us. In fact it was really good when things did go wrong! At least it gave us a different viewpoint and a different angle to go on, and it gave another couple a chance to shine.

'What was interesting is that people did improve on the tour. The people who were terrible were coming up and up and making fewer mistakes. Conversely, some of the people who were really good were starting to make errors, nightly, from lack of concentration. Denise Lewis, who was fabulous, would sometimes forget her steps. Or Zoe would get a step wrong, so you found out how consistent people were.'

Head judge Len was impressed by the way the dancers worked on the routines between shows.

'What was marvellous was that, as they were doing the same dances, their standard improved and most of them did take on board things that the judges said,' he says.

'We'd see them out the back and saying, "Len said I did the heel leads on that." Letitia was a good example because she did a pivot and her leg kept going up, which I commented on. The next time I saw it they'd cured it, which was great.'

While the atmosphere in the *Strictly* studio is always electric, the size of the arenas on tour meant that was magnified thirty-fold.

'The tour is very different in the respect that we have so many more people watching, so the audience reaction is so much louder and it feels that much more exciting,' says Ian Waite. 'When we dance at the studio the audience is only around 300, and this was 10,000 people at once. It was vast.'

Craig was delighted by the audience reaction and how well they joined in the fun – even if it meant more booing!

'I loved it and the audiences loved it,' he says. 'The tour really was about the audiences because people don't get to come to Television Centre, so it's great that they can go out and see how it's done. There are still cameras there and it is exactly like being in a studio audience on a Saturday night, but with a humungous amount of people. The energy in the arena is just mind-blowing!'

As always on tour, some dates mean more than others. For Arlene, it was a privilege to find herself at the MEN Arena in Manchester.

'I loved Manchester,' she explains. 'It happens to be my home town and I couldn't believe I was performing to thousands just around the corner from where I took my first dance class!'

Being on tour buses and in the same hotels meant that, for the first time in five series, the judges could really mingle with the celebrities and dancers.

'I really enjoyed that part of the tour,' says Craig. 'At the BBC, when we do the live show, we really don't mix with anyone. We come in at 6 p.m., do the show, and that's it. If we go to the BBC bar afterwards everyone is busy with their family and friends so there isn't much time to talk to them.

'On the tour, we were all living in the same hotel we had time to party together, go for meals and have a drink in the hotel bar. Some days you had the whole day off, so you could arrange lunch with someone and just socialise a lot more, which I loved. Of course the dancers could say things to us that they couldn't say before, so backstage they'd be saying, "Oh come on, give us a ten tonight!"'

Arlene also enjoyed spending time with the performers.

'It's strange getting to know both the dancers and celebs,' she says. 'We are so apart from them on the TV show, but we had an amazing group on the tour, hard working and committed. It was great to spend time with them.'

On stage, the show sparkled with all the glamour of the TV show, with glitter balls, beautiful frocks and sumptuous lighting. Backstage, says Craig, it's another matter.

'It was a tip,' he laughs. 'There were boxes, cables, everyone without make-up and wearing their normal rehearsal wear. The places we had to eat were hilarious. At one place there was just a curtain in the middle of a big space and it was like the worst naff caff you've ever seen. The food was always very good and the company that provided it were great, but it wasn't exactly candles and tablecloths.

'It was basic backstage living but most of us are used to that. I loved it though because it was such a good atmosphere and it brought everyone together. As bad as backstage is, and sometimes it was really cramped, with all the guys shoved into one room with one mirror, everyone seemed to muck in and get on with it.

'It's quite the antithesis of someone standing at the top of the stairs in their glittery outfit!'

Stage Entertainment and Phil McIntyre Entertainment in association with BBC Worldwide present

Strictly Come Dancing: The Live Tour!

For next year's tour details go to:
www.strictlycomedancinglive.co.uk

The dancers

Zoe Ball and Ian Waite
Letitia Dean and Darren Bennett
Matt Di Angelo and Flavia Cacace
Darren Gough and Lilia Kopylova
Denise Lewis and Matthew Cutler
Louisa Lytton and Vincent Simone
James Martin and Camilla Dallerup
Martin Offiah and Camilla Dallerup
Christopher Parker and Nicole Cutler

*The winners
(no. of shows won)*

Matt and Flavia – 16
Louisa and Vincent – 10
Darren and Lilia – 8
Zoe and Ian – 5
Letitia and Darren – 1

Chris *clowns about*

Those viewers who have been with the series from day one will be familiar with **Christopher Parker**'s unique brand of dance and, in particular, his unforgettable paso doble.

The former soap star, who leapt to fame as Spencer Moon in *EastEnders*, was not the most natural of hoofers but won the hearts of the nation in series one and shocked the judges when he made it through to the final.

Four years on he got the chance to re-create his matador moments on the tour and he was delighted.

'I really enjoyed the TV show, but at the time I was working hard on *EastEnders* as well,' he recalls. 'Being the first series, we didn't know that it would be so full on. We were told there would be five hours' training a week – and anyone who's done it knows that it's 25 hours at least! I'm really glad I took it on though. You don't really realize how much you enjoy it until it's finished and then it feels like there's a big hole in your life.

'I have nothing but fond memories of the series so it was really nice to dig out the shoes and put them on again. I never thought that I would need them again.'

With his original partner, Hanna Karttunen, no longer on the show, Chris had to learn his routines with professional Nicole Cutler. Before they started rehearsing, Chris made sure she understood what she was letting herself in for.

'I always wanted to finish *Strictly* on a high and I feel that I did,' he says. 'Natasha was the right winner but one of the biggest accomplishments in my career was getting to the final. I wasn't the best dancer, to put it mildly, so it goes to show that if you really try hard you can achieve things. I hope it also made a lot of people, who couldn't dance like me, think, Actually I'll give it a go.

'Hanna and I had tried to be as entertaining as possible. When I decided to do the tour, I sat down with Nicole and said, "We've got to do the paso because, four years on, I still walk down the street and people hold a coat up like a cape or say "I love your paso". Secondly, we have to be entertaining.'

'The standard had increased tenfold since I was on the show. The audience can watch Zoe's tango and well up with emotion, because it's a beautiful dance. We had to go out there and make them laugh. I didn't care if they were laughing at me, as long as they were having a good night out. Luckily, Nicole agreed with me.'

The couple had very little time to perfect their routine as both were on holiday just before the tour was due to start. In two weeks they had to learn five dances – two individual dances, two group dances and a finale.

'I'd had a few sessions with Nicole but we didn't have as much practice as we wanted to,' he says. 'And, of course, out of the whole tour I was the one who hadn't danced for the longest period of time, and I didn't have my original partner, so I was really up against it. I got off a flight from LA, walked into rehearsals two hours late, and I was terrified.'

Not surprisingly, when surrounded by the likes of Denise Lewis, Matt Di Angelo and Zoe Ball, Chris failed to top the leader board in any of the shows, and frequently drew a derogatory two from Craig. But he was having fun and, more to the point, so were the audience.

'I'm fine with the role of clown because I know I'm not a good dancer and as long as everyone is enjoying it, that's fine,' he says. 'It wasn't hard to take the judges' criticism because we all get on so well. I've known Arlene for many years, spent time with Len in LA and Craig I absolutely adore as well, even though we have this love–hate relationship. And I respect all three for their professional opinion.

'I had a lot less pressure than everyone else, because they're going out there to do these incredible dances and it's very easy for them to get it wrong. If I messed up it wasn't as big a deal – the audience laughed even harder so I didn't feel the pressure.'

Chris's paso was a sensation and even the judges started to appreciate his entertainment value.

'Len gave me a ten on two occasions,' laughs Chris. 'It felt really good. Night after night I was standing there getting a barrage of abuse and it was wonderful that Len threw me an olive branch.'

The paso went down so well with the crowd that, on one occasion Chris and his famous 'running with the cape' style made a lap of honour. That almost meant an early exit for him on one show.

'As I ran round I fell over,' he reveals. 'My ankle blew up and my whole foot was black and incredibly painful. I had to have MRI scans and then, because I was walking on it awkwardly, other parts of the foot started hurting. They put me in a moon-boot, like footballers wear, and I had to ice it all the time. I was told I shouldn't dance but the show must go on!'

To make each show unique, Chris and Matt dared each other to add a little extra to their routines.

'One night he said, "In your paso, when you stand there with your arms up, do a big hip thrust." I did it, and I'd never got such a huge laugh. Then I dared Matt and he did it too. I mentioned it during our conversation with the judges, on stage, and the audience loved it. Arlene wasn't impressed!'

Len came to the rescue when another unexpected incident interrupted the show.

'At one point a woman, who may have had a few too many, ran on to the stage and started dancing,' he reveals. 'Instead of calling security, Len danced her off the stage but, once he'd done that, he fell down the stairs and did a forward roll. He looked like James Bond!'

With eight shows a week, and travelling in between, the tour was tiring – but Chris isn't complaining.

'It was physically and mentally gruelling. I've run two London Marathons and this was right up there with those.

'But I had a brilliant time and, as you spend all day and night together for two months, you form these big bonds so I've made friends for life.'

Len on Chris

'For me, Chris Parker was the star of the tour. I thought he was absolutely great. I even gave him a ten one night! Technically it wasn't brilliant, the choreography wasn't brilliant but the pure entertainment value was fantastic. He hurt his foot really badly during the tour and they told him not to dance but he wouldn't give up. He came out and tried his hardest every time, knowing that Craig was going to give him a two, which takes a lot of doing.

'You've also got to admire the professionals too. Nicole would come out in the paso doble, with all those silly antics of Chris, and still try as though she were dancing with a world champion. It doesn't matter how poor their celebrity is the professionals still come out and give 100 per cent.'

Cherie Lunghi

Cherie Lunghi can't wait to get her dancing shoes on and says she never stops moving: 'I've danced on beaches, boats, you name it! I'm very happy when I'm dancing and I'm not very good at sitting still – I'm on the right show, aren't I!'

The elegant actress has been a leading lady of stage and screen since bursting on to the scene in *Excalibur,* along with Helen Mirren, in 1981. She has had a regular recurring role in *Casualty* and *Casualty 1906* as well as starring in *Waking the Dead, The Inspector Lynley Mysteries, Secret Diary of a Call Girl* and *The Manageress,* where she played a female football manager. She is also instantly recognizable from a series of popular coffee ads!

Partner: James Jordan

Cherie's original ambition was to be a ballet dancer but at the age of 11 she was enrolled at the Arts Educational Trust School in Hyde Park, London – a stage school attended by fellow pupils Nigel Havers, Jenny Agutter and Jane Seymour. Cherie says the school was creative and inspiring but without pretensions, unlike some 'pushy showbizzy stage schools'.

At 24, she joined the Royal Shakespeare Company, where she worked with stage legends Dame Judi Dench and Sir Ian McKellen.

Cherie took ballet classes when she was younger and feels this may help with her posture in the dances. 'I think doing a bit of ballet has given me poise,' she says. 'And my job as an actor may help because I have had to perform a few dancing and ballet scenes on the odd occasion.'

The actress, who has a 22-year-old daughter, agreed to take part in *Strictly* because she believes it will be 'tremendous fun'. Having grown up watching Ginger Rogers and Fred Astaire she is instinctively drawn to ballroom, because of the romantic nature of the dance.

Last year's series had Cherie glued to the box and she is a great admirer of the professional dancers. 'I love watching the emotional journeys and transformations,' she says. 'And I love *Strictly* because it is not a cruel show. Everyone's trying their best and the public are very supportive.

'Personally the dancers to me are up there with the standard of ballet dancers. I have nothing but the utmost of respect for them!'

Cherie's hoping she won't forget any of her routines, and will be relying on partner James if she does. 'James is wonderful and I know he will carry me through!'

And, believe it or not, she is hoping she gets an attack of nerves before she hits the dance floor. 'You never really get over first-night nerves,' she explains. 'And in a way, first-night nerves are necessary because you need the adrenalin to make you want to do well. Once I didn't have any first-night nerves and I had a very bad first night!'

Dancing is a great way to build physical activity into our lives. Regular exercise can improve the condition of the heart and lungs, as well as test our balance. Dancing is a brilliant way to burn calories and you'll enjoy yourself so much you'll forget you're exercising! You will develop skills like poise, grace and better coordination as you learn to glide across the dance floor, and let's not forget the sense of achievement you'll feel as you master the most complex moves. As well as exercising your body, regular dancing will help keep your mind active, by improving oxygen circulation to the brain and working your memory by remembering complex steps. All in all, dancing can make you a happier, fitter, sexier and much more confident person!

To dance for any length of time requires muscular endurance and motor fitness. Start slowly, build up your stamina over time, and always warm up and cool down when dancing to avoid injury. Please be sure to check with your doctor before starting any exercise programme.

WARM UP

First move: **punch**

- Start with feet wider than hip distance apart, both hands on hips. Keep your back straight, your tummy held in and your shoulders back, making fists with your hands. (1)
- Punch up with your right arm; grab and pull back with the left arm. (2)
- Repeat the move, punching up four times, three across your body, and two down, and then repeat with the other arm.

Second move: **knee lift**

- Start with your feet wider than hip distance apart. (1)
- Put your hands on your hips. Bring your left knee up, twisting your torso to the left. (2)
- Bring your foot back to the starting position.
- Repeat twice on each leg.

Third move: **step and lunge**

- From a standing position, bring your right leg across your body, lunging forward. Make sure your right knee does not go in front of your toe. Grasp your arms above your head as you go into the lunge, and stretch. **(1)**
- Go back to the start position, and then take three steps to the side. **(2, 3, 4)**
- Repeat the move, lunging with your left leg. Repeat this sequence four times.

Fourth move: **side step out**

- Start with your feet hip distance apart.
- Take a wide step to the right, and lunge sideways with your right leg. Bring your left arm forward and your right arm backwards. Keep them both straight and at shoulder height. Hold your tummy in and turn your torso to the right. **(1)**
- Step out of the lunge and march on the spot, bringing your legs back together. **(2)**
- Repeat in the opposite direction, lunging with your left leg. Repeat this sequence four times. **(3, 4)**

TANGO

Use a chair for balance throughout

First move: **ochos**

1

- First do three forward ochos: rest both hands on the chair back. On tiptoes, step forward with your right foot. **(1)**
- Sweep your left foot round and across to the right. Follow the direction of your foot with your hips, turning your body to the right. **(2)**
- With your weight on your left foot, sweep round your right foot, stepping across to the left and turning your hips to the left as you step. **(1)**
- Sweep your left foot around and across to the right, bringing your feet together to finish. **(3)**
- Repeat the move again.

- Now do three backward ochos: starting with your feet together, step back and to the right with your left foot. **(1)**
- Sweep your right foot around and backwards to the left. **(2)**
- Sweep the left foot around and step backwards to the right. **(3)**
- Sweep the right foot around and finish with your feet together. **(4)**
- Follow with another set of forward ochos. Repeat the sequence four times.

1

2

3

4

Second move: **standing kick backs**

- Stand with your weight on your right foot, left foot pointing forward, and your right arm on your hip. **(1)**
- With your left hand holding on to the chair, step forward lightly with your left foot but keeping the weight on your right leg. Cross your left leg over your right leg. When your knees connect, lift your left foot off the floor, bending your knee and hooking your left leg around your right leg. **(2)**
- Repeat this move three times in a controlled movement.
- Next step forward with your left foot and swivel the right foot round, so that your body is now facing the opposite direction and your right hand is holding the chair. **(3, 4)**
- Repeat the kick-back move with your other leg four times. **(5)**

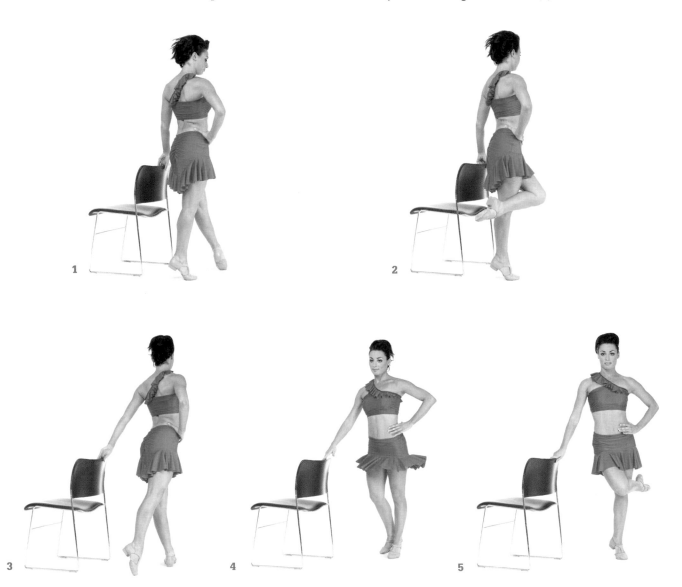

Third move: **tango ab crunch**

- Sitting on the chair, start with your knees together, toes pointed to the floor and your stomach held in. **(1)**
- Grasp the sides of the chair. Lift your right leg up over your left leg, bringing your left leg a couple of inches off the floor. **(2)**

1

2

- Point your toe and straighten your right leg, twisting your torso to the right. **(3)**
- As you turn to the right, straighten your left leg and cross it over your right knee. **(4, 5)**

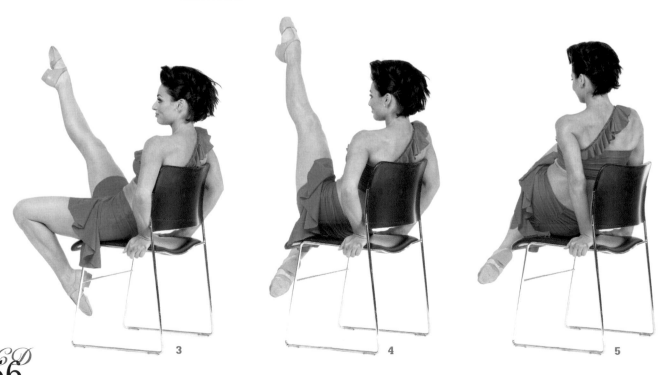

3

4

5

- Repeat on the other side: start by crossing your left leg over your right.
- Repeat the move again in each direction. **(6, 7)**

Fourth move: **hero**

- Stand with your hands on your hips. **(1)**
- Moving anticlockwise around the chair, step forward with your left foot. **(2)**
- Pivot on your left foot, turning anticlockwise on the spot and step round to the right. **(3)**
- Pivot on your right foot, stepping back, around the chair, with your left foot. **(4)**
- Brush your right foot past your left foot, and step right. This will take you back to the start position. **(5, 6)**
- Repeat again, starting with left foot forward.

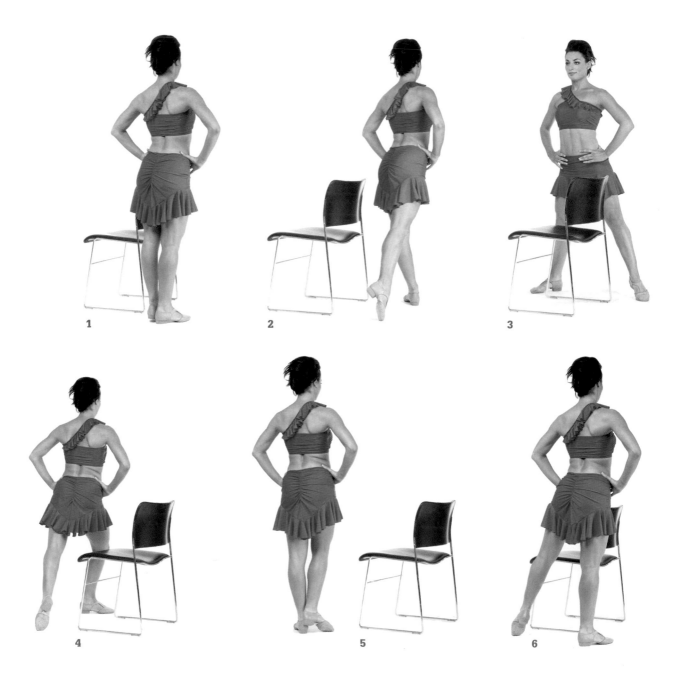

1   2   3

4   5   6

- When you get to the final position, step on to the right leg, then slightly sway back to the left. **(7, 8)**
- Now repeat clockwise around the chair, leading with the right leg. **(9 –14)**
- Repeat again and then change direction.

7

8

9

10

11

12

13

14

SALSA

First move: basic step

- Keep your arms soft and relaxed. **(1)**
- Step forward with your left foot. Rock back on to your right foot. **(2, 3)**
- Bring your left foot back to meet your right foot. Shift your weight on to the opposite leg. **(4)**

 1

 2

 3

 4

- Repeat, but this time step back on to the right foot. **(5)**
- Rock forward on to the left foot, bringing your right foot back to meet your left foot, changing weight to opposite leg. **(6)**
- Repeat once, slowly and twice slightly faster.

 5

 6

Second move: **salsa swivels**

- Stand straight on tiptoes. Sweep your left foot forward and across, stepping to the right and slightly twisting your body to the left. At the same time bring both arms up to shoulder height. **(1)**
- Bring your right foot to meet your left foot, taking you back to the starting position, remaining on tiptoes. Bring your right arm back over your head (as if brushing your hair). **(2)**
- Then bring arms back out to the side. **(3)**
- Repeat four times, starting with your left foot and then four times with your right foot.

Third move: **twist and jump**

- Stand on your right leg, left leg pointing behind. Arms straight. **(1)**
- Twist to the right, tapping your left foot to your right foot. **(2)**
- Twist to the left, pointing your toes up and pushing your left heel out. **(3)**
- Bring your hands to your waist and tap your left foot behind your right foot. **(4)**

- Lift your left knee up and raise your arms above your head in a small controlled jump. **(5)**
- Step back with your left foot, bringing your arms down. **(6)**
- Step sideways with your right foot so that you are standing with your feet hip width apart.
- Step forward with your left foot ready to repeat the sequence on the other side. **(7, 8)**
- Repeat twice in each direction.

Fourth move: **twist and shimmy**

- Stand with weight on your right foot, left knee slightly bent and hands by your side. **(1)**
- Take a step forward with your left foot and bring your arms up and behind your head. **(2)**
- Step forward on to your right foot, bringing your arms down. Spin round on your right foot finishing with your feet together. **(3, 4, 5)**
- Step back with your right foot, rock forward on to your left foot and finish with your feet together, changing weight. Shimmy your shoulders throughout this move. **(6, 7)**
- Repeat the sequence until you get to **(5)**. This time rock back on to your left foot and tap your right foot to your left foot. This will make you ready to step forward with the right foot in order to repeat the move in the opposite direction.
- Repeat once slowly and twice a little faster.

COOL DOWN

First move: **the relax squat**

- Stand with your feet slightly wider than hip distance apart. Hold your arms above your head. **(1)**
- Squat down keeping your back straight, making sure your knees do not go beyond your toes and that your bottom is parallel to the floor. If you can, put your hands flat on floor. **(2, 3)**
- Straighten your knees and slowly straighten your back, uncurling your spine and raising your head last of all, until you are back in the start position. **(4)**
- Repeat this sequence twice.

Second move: **curtsy tricep stretch**

- Stand with feet hip distance apart. Point your right foot ready to do a clockwise turn in three steps starting with the right foot. **(1)** The arms assist the turn. On the third step, take your arms up, point with your left foot. **(2)**
- Bring your left foot back into a curtsy. At the same time, bring your left arm back and grasp your left elbow with your right arm, gently stretching your tricep. **(3)**
- Hold for 10 seconds and then repeat with the opposite arm.

Third move: **waist stretch**

- Stand with your feet slightly wider than hip distance apart. Hold your tummy in. Bring your right arm over your head, and your left arm down. **(1)**
- Bend sideways from the waist and hold for 10 seconds. Repeat once on each side. **(2, 3)**

Fourth move: *Strictly* **calf stretch**

- Stand with your feet hip distance apart. Take a big step forward with your right leg into a lunge, pushing your left heel down to the floor. Clasp your arms above your head. Hold for 10 seconds. **(1)**
- Go back to the start position and then repeat on the other side. **(2)**

Erin Boag

New Zealand dancer **Erin** has earned herself the nickname of Miss Whiplash, due to her tough teaching methods on the programme. The daughter of professional dancers, Erin started to learn at a very young age.

'I guess like many little girls, I wanted to dance!' she remembers. 'Mum took me as a three year old to dance classes where I began learning ballet, tap, jazz, ballroom and Latin. Through my teens, I was a really keen sportsgirl – I can tell you I was a really kick-ass swimmer!'

At 15, she travelled to Australia to watch a big competition and decided, on the spot, that competing was her future. At 18, she was the New Zealand 10 Dance Amateur champion. But the road to stardom was not easy, and there was plenty of hardship along the way. After paying a deposit on a flat, Erin and her partner had £120 and ate a lot of beans on toast.

'One memory that sticks in my mind is sitting on a bus with my last pound in my hand not knowing whether to laugh or cry,' says Erin. 'I think this experience made me more determined; it helped me appreciate life more too.'

In 1997, she met Anton. A year later they danced at the Royal Albert Hall and were placed in the top 50.

'As we walked on to the floor I cried, thinking I'd finally made it,' says Erin. 'And that all the hard work, sweat and tears were worth it.'

After turning professional in 2002, they came third in the British National Dance championships at Blackpool.

Although she has been with *Strictly Come Dancing* since it began Erin has yet to win the trophy, but she has come tantalizingly close. She was fourth in series one with rugby player Martin Offiah, and third in series two with Julian Clary. In series three, Erin danced with Colin Jackson and got to one of the closest finals ever seen on the programme.

'Colin was an absolute star and I believe the best male celebrity to ever appear on *Strictly Come Dancing*,' Erin recalls. 'As a partner he will be tough to beat.'

Speciality: Ballroom
Professional Achievements: IDTA Classic Champion; British National Finalist; BDF Star Ball Finalist; UK & International Rising Star Finalist; UBC Canadian Champion

Flavia Cacace

Like her dance partner Vincent Simone, **Flavia** was born in Italy but her family moved to Surrey when she was four. It was there, at a local dance school, that she was to meet Vincent 12 years later. 'It's a complete coincidence that we are both from Italy, as we met in the UK,' she says.

Flavia, who is one of six children, was an instant hit on the dance floor, and steadily worked her way through the junior medals until an impressed tutor suggested she compete instead. At 12, she found a dance partner, but, as he came from several miles away, she had to rely on her parents for numerous lifts.

'Mum and Dad spent so long taxing me around to rehearse with my partner,' she says. 'I really couldn't have done it without them as they supported me both financially and mentally.'

After two years of competitions her partner decided to hang up his dancing shoes and a new partnership lasted only a year, as time pressures and GCSEs got in the way.

Flavia's prayers were answered when Vincent started at the same dance school. The chemistry was instant and, in 2001, they turned professional and began teaching at the Dance World, the very studio where they met.

Flavia's experiences on *Strictly* have gone from one extreme to the other. Her first celebrity partner was Jimmy Tarbuck who, unfortunately, had to bow out early.

In series five, Flavia transformed Matt Di Angelo from a shy, nervous dancer to a 'matinee idol' and a worthy finalist.

'Matt really gave it his all and there is no more you can ask than that,' says Flavia.

'Matt was genuinely devastated when things went wrong, and that happened a few times. He put himself under pressure to do well for me. Making the final alone made me as happy as if we'd won.'

Speciality: Ten Dance/Argentine tango
Professional Achievements: UK Professional Ten Dance Champions; UK Professional Show Dance Champions; UK Argentine Tango Show Champions; World Argentine Tango Show Champions; World and European Ten Dance and Showdance Finalist

Camilla Dallerup

Born in Aalborg, Denmark, where she lived until she was 16, **Camilla** had only just learnt to walk before she was dancing. Her mother enrolled her in a class when she was just two because she thought it would teach her good posture and nice manners.

'I suppose at the beginning I was just like any other kid who wanted to be outside playing instead of going dancing,' she recalls. 'That was until the day my mum said: "OK, fine, no more dancing"… I was then hooked because now it was my choice.'

Along with a lad named Taupin, Camilla entered her first competition at six, lying about her age because contestants were supposed to be eight and over! Although she trained at a stage school, she dropped singing and acting after winning the Junior Danish Championships at 12 to concentrate on ballroom and Latin. Her ever supportive parents brought her to the UK twice a year to compete in the UK Junior Blackpool Competitions.

As she grew older, the Danish beauty studied business, law and finance to become a real-estate agent in Denmark. Still competing on the amateur circuit, she worked full time to pay for lessons and costumes and trained in the evenings.

In 1996 she met Brendan Cole and they shared eight years as a dance partnership.

'I had the most amazing competitive years with Brendan – four years in amateur and then four very successful years as professional. I have some very wonderful memories, of succeeding and performing all over the world.'

Her most successful *Strictly* dance partner to date was Gethin Jones.

'He started slowly but then, oh, boy! He was magnificent!'

Speciality: Latin American
Professional Achievements: Asia Pacific Latin American Champion; New Zealand Latin American Champion; World Open Latin Dance Semi-Finalist; International Open Latin Dance Semi-Finalist; British Open Latin Dance Semi-Finalist

Karen Hardy

Karen's *Strictly* highlight was undoubtedly her series four win with cricketer Mark Ramprakash. Dancing with Mark was, she says, 'the most wonderful experience ever' and he is 'a true sportsman in every way. He expects nothing but the best from himself and will not stop until he is happy. He took an amazing journey from being very quiet and reserved to allowing himself to be caught up in our world of dance and really experience (I hope) a memorable time.'

Originally from Bournemouth, Karen attended two dance schools as a child – the Gaiety School of Dancing and the Nice 'n' Easy Dance Studios, run by respected teacher and judge Lynette Boyce.

Initially, dancing was something to do at the weekend, 'just as fun with my friends'. She loved the sequins, frocks, and make-up giving everything 'a sense of occasion', which she thinks is lacking from everyday life. But she didn't take her hobby too seriously until she won her first medal. 'It was then I decided to be a dancer – I loved winning!'

At 18, Karen moved to the States where she excelled in the amateur ranks, winning numerous American amateur championships. In 1994 she and dance partner Brian Watson turned professional and competed for five years.

Karen joined *Strictly* in series three, partnering injury-prone newsreader Bill Turnbull. After the glory of victory in series four, Karen was brought back down to earth in series five, when she and actor Brian Capron were first to leave.

'Brian was a gentleman,' she says. 'It was an honour and a pleasure to dance with Brian and I wish we could have taken our journey further.'

Speciality: Latin American
Professional Achievements: World Masters Champion; International Open to the World Champion; United Kingdom Open to the World Champion; British National Champion; Open Italian Champion

Mark Foster

Olympian Mark Foster will be going for gold in this year's *Strictly Come Dancing*. The veteran swimmer went into training days after returning from Beijing, where he competed in his fifth Olympic games. In recognition of this prodigious feat, Team GB voted for him to carry the British flag in the opening ceremony, an accolade for which he feels 'extremely honoured'.

Competing has been a way of life for Mark for nearly 20 years, since he won a National Championship competition aged 11. At 15, he was selected for the British swimming team and he won his first international medal the following year at the Commonwealth Games in Edinburgh as part of England's 100m freestyle relay team.

Partner: Hayley Holt

Since then he has won six World Championships, 10 European Champion medals and two Commonwealth Champion medals and broken no fewer than eight world records.

A back injury forced Mark to quit international competitions in 2006 but, after a break of 18 months, he was back in the pool, claiming two titles in National Championships. Mark qualified for the 2008 Beijing games after winning the 50m freestyle final at the British Championships in Sheffield. Seconds before the start of the final disaster struck when the zip on his swimsuit popped open but, in a flash, Mark stripped out of his costume and competed in the bottoms he had on underneath. Such quick thinking under pressure is bound to come in handy on the Saturday-night shows.

Amazingly, Mark's dad couldn't swim but he was determined that his children would feel safe in the water so he booked them all swimming lessons at a young age – a move that clearly paid off.

Shy Mark, who stands a lean 6 foot 6 inches, describes himself as a typical bloke dancer. 'I've never been to any classes and I only dance when I've had a few beers at weddings or in clubs,' he says.

Mark watched his friend and former training partner Colin Jackson get as far as the final in 2005, and hopes he can do just as well – if not better.

'I'd love to win,' he says. 'But I'm a realist and I know that a lot of work needs to be done and many hours need to be spent training if I'm going to make the final at Christmas.'

His biggest fear is being eliminated in the first week. He is also worried about forgetting the routine but he is hoping that the whole experience will help him battle his shyness.

'I am very self-conscious,' he says. 'But I hope that doesn't hold me back from putting in the best performance I possibly can during *Strictly*.'

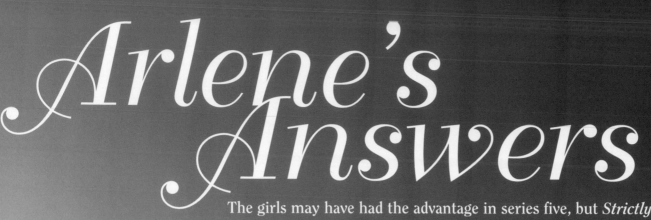

Arlene's Answers

The girls may have had the advantage in series five, but *Strictly*'s first lady Arlene Phillips was backing the lads. She had a soft spot for both Gethin Jones and Matt Di Angelo and saw their potential from day one. After a tasty tango from Gethin and a jubilant jive from Matt in week three, she announced: 'The boys are back in town – they're in it to win it. I'm loving Gethin and Matt and John, they're going to show us something. I'm convinced of that.'

With Gethin in third place and Matt coming a close second to Alesha in the final, Arlene was right on the nose. Here's her round-up of the highs and lows of the series.

Most Impressive Start

Kelly Brook got off to a flying start and I loved her rumba, the first individual dance with Brendan. Her tango was amazing, so dramatic and emotional. I told her she was the kind of dancer I'd like to wrap up in cotton wool to preserve her and perhaps I should have done because the two weeks after that, with the illegal lifts and the role-reversal paso, lost her some valuable points. But it was a shame she had to leave when she did because she was getting back on track and would have gone far.

Biggest Surprise

Gethin Jones when he went from the timid, unsure dancer we saw at the beginning to a fantastic, graceful leading man. His improvement was incredible and by the end of the series he really was Glorious Gethin.

Most Improvement

The transformation in Matt Di Angelo was incredible. He looked scared to go near Flavia in his week-one cha-cha-cha, but I could see that he had a lot of potential. He proved me right. By the time he did the American smooth in week four, he looked and danced like a star.

Best Performance

Alesha Dixon and Matthew Cutler had so many perfect performances on the show but I would have to choose their waltz. They scored a ten from me the first time they danced it and again in the final. It really is one of the best ballroom performances we've ever seen. Breathtaking.

Voted out too soon

Gabby Logan had such a lot of potential and, with her gymnastic background, could really put on a show. It was a shame to see her go so early.

Stayed Too Long

Dominic Littlewood seemed to have a problem with the timing and rhythm, which spoiled his routines. He also had a problem with us judges and didn't believe a word we said. He was annoying because he didn't want to hear the truth.

Best Overall Dancer

For my money, Jill Halfpenny remains the best Latin dancer we've seen. Who could forget that astonishing, energetic jive! Alesha pips them all to the post at ballroom but, as an all-rounder, I would say Darren Gough has the lead.

Worst Overall Dancer

It has to be the sweet, but rhythmically challenged Christopher Parker. His disastrous paso doble, which I have watched many times on the *Strictly* tour, is the worst I've ever seen – but at least he's entertaining with it.

Quotes:

On Gethin's Viennese waltz:
'Tonight you were Gethin the Gallant. Romantic, strong. Camilla, you were melting in his arms like whipped cream in a coffee.'

To Kelly after her Viennese waltz:
'Beauty and the Beast have danced right back into the fairy tale.'

To Matt in week one, after he danced to the Tom Jones' hit 'Mama Told Me Not to Come':
'This mama says you should be here, on this floor, and improving every week.'

On John Barnes' jive:
'I know she's small but you're hanging over her like sloppy seconds.'

On Kate Garraway's samba:
'More like a dancing quail than a dancing queen.'

On Matt Di Angelo's American smooth:
'Matt, can I call you Matinee Idol? That was a sensational smooth.'

Craig's Critique

Craig Revel Horwood was amazed at the standard of the celebrity dancers in series five – or at least half of them!

'There was a real divide this time,' he recalls. 'Half the celebrities were really good dancers and the other half were really bad. That divide made it so difficult to judge, because it was rather obvious who should stay and who should go. Of course, that narrowed down as time went on.'

As the series kicked off the ladies definitely had the edge, and Craig was impressed with all the female celebs, for different reasons.

'Penny was up for the challenge and really gave it her all so she was a really big contender,' he says. 'Gabby didn't get far enough into the series to show what she could really do – the big dances where she could use her acrobatics. Kate was brilliant, because she was such fun. I've never seen anyone with such a lack of ability get through as amazingly as she did!'

Best dancer at the start

Kelly Brook was the one who caught my attention in the beginning because of her personality. For me, Alesha ran a very close second to Kelly at the start, but I felt that Kelly was a brilliant all-rounder. It wasn't until we started seeing both of them over a period of time that we discovered Alesha was the best all-rounder. If Kelly had stayed there would have been a battle in the end and I imagine that their scores would have been pretty much on a par.

Worst dancer at the start

I expected Willie to be pretty bad but actually he wasn't too shabby at the ballroom stuff. Kate and Anton, sadly, were the worst. I think that's why Anton was getting a little bit frustrated and arguing with the judges. We've never see that side of Anton – it

was the first time he's shown his Brendan Cole-ness! I think having a challenging partner is good for a dancer. They have to be very creative and think about the choreography more.

Most improved

Letitia Dean made the biggest improvement. When she started she was totally lacking in confidence. The ability was there but I think her nerves were making her scream inside, especially when it came to the Latin stuff. When she gained confidence she really started to improve.

Biggest surprise

Gethin Jones was a real surprise. Every week he improved enormously. As his confidence grew, he started really enjoying it and getting into it a lot more. He blossomed, totally put the acting side into the dance, which makes the audience at home believe in what you're doing. The audience want to see the person being challenged – to see someone who couldn't do it, turn into a dancer. That gives everybody who has two left feet hope!

Shock exit

Gabby was definitely the biggest shock because she was good, and I thought she was very watchable. There were plenty of other people who should have been in that dance off, if it were down to talent. I'd liked to have seen her dance a bit more but, as we know from past experience, anyone in the middle of the leader board generally gets knocked out. You want to be either at the top or at the bottom but it's a hard thing to control. Even the judges can't control that. You're either liked or you're not. You can be absolutely phenomenal as a dancer and get knocked out.

Best sport

Kate was brilliant. She was like her colleague Fiona Phillips when she was on the show. She followed in Fiona's footsteps brilliantly! I know Kate was in an enormous amount of pain at the beginning. She couldn't walk, she was on crutches, then she had a shoulder injury but she still fought on. She listened to what we said and tried to get through it, without complaining. Good on her!

Kenny and Gabby

I think the fact that they were married went against them. It was odd that Kenny was favoured over Gabby, because she was clearly the better dancer. I think Kenny was loved for his robustness. He didn't care if he was bad, he was going to do his best. The fact that they were dancing with husband and wife team James and Ola made the exchanges on the show interesting but I don't think it helped. It's good television though!

Quotes:

On Alesha's final paso doble:
'Attack, passion, drama, I loved it.'

On Matt:
'Matt and Flavia always excite me.'

On Dominic Littlewood's cha cha cha:
'That was camper than this show, actually.'

After Arlene told John Barnes to get fit:
'I see a lot of potential here. I cannot agree with Arlene – I do like a man with a bit of meat on him!'

On Willie Thorne's tango:
'You were hunching over Erin like a walrus.'

On Kenny Logan's samba:
'That was complete dance disaster. It was grotesque in places. The hip thrusts were repulsive!'

On John Barnes salsa:
'One word. Re-spect!'

Costume designer Su Judd had plenty of glamorous ladies to dress in series five, from the leggy Penny Lancaster-Stewart and athletic Gabby Logan to diva Stephanie Beacham and the buxom Kelly Brook.

Strictly Stunning

As always, Su invited the celebrities to bring in pictures or magazine pages of styles that they would like to try and she got some interesting responses from the latest batch of dance novices.

'Kelly brought in pictures of old Hollywood stars and, coincidentally, I had brought in lots of Monroe pictures, because I already knew her and her style preferences,' says Su.

'Penny was really interesting because she's the first person who brought in her actual wardrobe! She brought all her favourite dresses, which was a great way of showing us what works for her body and what doesn't. Having been a model for years, she knows what suits her so she would say, "Here's my Versace dress. I like this length and the way it fits here ..."'

After Su and the designers have seen the pictures, they sit down with each celebrity and discuss the ideas, explain the technical requirements of each dance, and create a dress among them.

The designs then become a reality with the help of specialist outfitters Chrisanne and DSI.

'Kelly is fabulous to dress,' reveals Su. 'Alesha is an absolute dream because she came in with so many great ideas, and loved the whole process. Both she and Kelly absolutely loved it. It was a really good year for us because Gabby was amazing as well, has a great figure to work with and is really stylish, so it was nice to do something more grown up for her.'

Actress Stephanie Beacham, who was sadly the first woman out of the competition, came with very definite ideas on how to add a touch of Hollywood glamour.

'Stephanie Beacham was a diva – but in the best possible way,' says Su. 'She's a Hollywood great and she knows exactly what she wants, how things should fit; she knows her fashion and she knows everything about the way garments are made and how it works with her body. In a way, that makes it easy because she gives you very clear instructions but it also makes it difficult to be free thinking because she's quite set in her ways.

'She didn't have too many outfits but she was one of the few people that we have accepted for whom we wouldn't pre-design all her dresses. Normally they're designed before the show starts but for her we decided to make them slowly as the weeks went on, and she was happy to do as many fittings as we needed. She gave up plenty of time for that. She'd rather look good in the dress than at the dance, I think.

'The dress she liked the most was the one that we made for the initial photographs, which was just nude with loads of diamanté thrown at it. Out of everyone she pulled that idea off the best; we even diamantéd her shoes for her, which started a bit of a craze among the others.'

Favourite outfits
Kelly's Beauty and the Beast dress
Programme 6: Viennese waltz

Kelly looked so much more elegant in the ballroom dresses. People expected her to suit the raunchy dresses best but I think she looked beautiful in the ballroom dresses. When she first put on this lovely yellow dress, she was so excited she ran around the building at Chrisanne's and showed the whole design team there. It was six o'clock, so they were getting ready to go home, and it was a great way to end their day. All the machinists got to see it before it was on screen, so that was great.

The contestants can buy the dresses but they're all sold on, to make the money back, but Kelly didn't get this one. It would have cost her about £1800 to £2000 to buy.

Letitia's waltz dress
Programme 10: Waltz

Letitia Dean's waltz dress marked a real turning-point for her. She came out in the nude dress with the turquoise bodice and even Arlene was saying, 'Tonight, you look beautiful and you danced like a star.' Len said, 'You have never looked so lovely.' That was a real boost for her because she felt that she was beautiful and people were saying she was.

We had to fit Letitia weekly, so she came in every Monday, because she got thinner and thinner every week. She was never fat but she doesn't know how lovely she is, so it was difficult for her. We were fitting the dresses and having to remake them every week, taking fabric out, purely because she was dancing all the time. Within the first four weeks she lost loads of weight.

It's a common occurrence on *Strictly*, because everyone is getting so much exercise but Letitia, particularly, changed. Her legs are perfect and she always wanted to show them but that was a bit of a battle because short things don't make you look slim. But we try to make our celebs happy and we would often be shortening Letitia's dresses on the day.

Kenny's kilt
Programme 5: Paso doble

As soon as I met Kenny I said, 'Please can I do a kilt?' I had seen actor Alan Cumming wearing a gold kilt in the Edinburgh festival, where he was playing Dionysus that season. I took a picture of him to Kenny the first time we met, and said, 'How do you fancy something like this?' He was so into it, straight away, so we starting making it. Then it was just a case of working out which dance would be best. We were originally going to do it for a ballroom dance, with a dinner jacket, but the ballroom dancers were a bit upset at the thought of seeing so much of his legs and we thought it might have taken the elegance away. That's why we switched to the paso doble.

There was a slight malfunction there because Kenny had a pair of lucky pants, and he wouldn't go on without them! Obviously, well-worn white pants he'd been wearing for five weeks, every week, didn't go well with the kilt, so we had black pants over the top of them, which were supposed to cover everything. On the night, they came out the bottom and could be seen on the screen. I was

sitting at home going, 'Nooooo! You can see his pants!'

Alesha's jive dress
Programme 3: Jive

Alesha just looked amazing in everything. My favourite was the lime-green jive dress. It was shorts as opposed to a dress, so it was a playsuit. Alesha had seen one that Karen Hardy had worn on a DVD and playsuits were also around on the catwalks. She loved them, so she asked for that. It worked really well for the dance.

too. We had to sew real bras into all her outfits and, on reflection, the top half had too much block and didn't look as nice onscreen as it did offscreen. But I think the boys liked it because her middle was out and her legs were out! She looked brilliant whatever she wore but it's probably my least favourite dress of the series.

Brace yourself

On show three we had 'braces-gate' because Dominic's braces pinged off and James Jordan's went too. It's a problem because the braces are a key design in the jive and the dancers like that as a look. Normally, they are sewn on but, somehow or other, that was overlooked and it was a real shame. They both carried on but it does put them off their dancing. James actually pulled them off and threw them into the audience, but he managed it without losing his step.

Wardrobe malfunctions are my absolute dread but they happen less and less now because we've learned from the four series before. In series four we had the Karen and Mark disaster, when they got tangled up in the microphones, and Lilia has also lost her microphone in the past, so we now sew them into the costumes.

Penny's samba outfit
Programme 4: Samba

We try not to be too themed in our outfits, like the American show is, but something always comes up. Penny and Ian were dancing to 'These Boots are Made for Walking' and asked us for those boots just a week before the show. We'd done a little gold dress already so we cut another three inches off it and the sequins made the boots. They are actually made out of lycra and literally lasted for one dance. They're hideous things but they looked great onscreen. The week before the samba, Penny asked to be voted back in by the public so she could wear them. Luckily she made it through.

Least favourite outfit

Brendan was very happy with Kelly and liked her in all the dresses we gave her, apart from one. He hated the green samba dress she wore in show eight and I think Kelly did

Brendan's pink shoes

For their week-seven jive, Brendan asked me as a joke to give him pink diamanté shoes that would match Kelly's dress. I think he was trying to annoy me but I said, 'OK, that'll be great.' When he got them he was so pleased and the viewers loved them. We got letters from so many people, a lot of them asking where you can get them. The problem with them is that they don't last. They're not like the glitter ones that appeared on the catwalk later, which you can now buy cheaper version of for men. These were Swarovski encrusted so, as he danced, the crystals came off. They were all put on by hand and there were probably more than 1000 crystals on each shoe.

Heather Small

M People diva Heather Small will be searching 'for the hero inside herself' and hoping she can make herself 'proud' when she takes to the dance floor. The London-born singer started her career with a group called Hot House, which brought her to the attention of Mike Pickering, a DJ at Manchester's legendary Haçienda nightclub. Impressed by her vocal talents, he invited her to his studio to hear some songs he'd written with her in mind. M People (Mike's People) was born.

The group was to make her one of the most iconic voices of the nineties, with such hits as 'Moving On Up', 'One Night In Heaven' and 'Search For The Hero'. M People landed the Best British Dance Act Award at the Brits in 1994 and 1995, as well as the Mercury Music Prize for the album, *Elegant Slumming*.

Partner: Brian Fortuna

After becoming a solo artist in 2000, Heather released the album *Proud* and the single of the same name. It was to become an anthem for many national celebrations, including Britain's successful Olympic bid, the sixtieth anniversary of VE day and the England's victory in the 2003 Rugby World Cup.

Mum-of-one Heather was persuaded to take part by her family when she was about to turn it down. 'Everyone said to me, "C'mon, Heather, you love to dance, give it a go!"' she says. 'So I thought why not?'

As a pop singer, she is a natural dancer who feels she will gravitate towards the Latin but is looking forward to learning ballroom.

'It's so elegant – the whole straight back and having to have your head in the right position,' she explains. 'There's a real sense of achievement with learning something like ballroom.'

Amazingly, although she had performed in front of massive crowds throughout her career, Heather suffers from bouts of stage fright.

'I keep thinking it'll get better but sometimes I feel like scurrying away and just hiding,' she admits. 'I'm hoping that throwing myself into the deep end will help, even though I know I will be very nervous.'

Another worry is that she is not very good at taking criticism, so she's not looking forward to hearing the judges' verdicts.

At the moment Heather isn't thinking about winning – all she can think about is cracking the dances: 'There is such a beauty in dancing – it's like singing,' she says. 'There's a real achievement in doing it and doing it well. I've already thought to myself that after the show I'm definitely going to keep it up.'

Although she is looking forward to learning the dances, Heather is aware that good footwork is not always enough to save a celeb from the public vote. 'If the public don't like you, you'll be out! That's just hit me and that's quite a sobering thought!'

Kate Garraway

'I'll let you into a secret – I actually thought I was going be fabulous!'

It was third time lucky for the *Strictly* producers when they bagged Kate Garraway for series five. The first time she was asked she was pregnant and the second time was too soon after the birth of daughter Darcey, so she had to decline.

'When they asked again I thought, Nobody gets asked out on a date three times! I'd better do it this time or they'll never ask again,' she says.

'Watching at home as a viewer I was so envious, and I thought I would love to do that, so when the chance came along this time I bit the hand off.'

Bursting with enthusiasm Kate threw herself into the challenge, only to be thwarted in early rehearsals by a painful tendon injury that put her out of the group dance in the first show. When she finally got back into the competition, her scores limped. Bottom of the leader board in all but one week, she even managed to score a two from Craig for her stumbling samba.

'I'll let you into a secret – I actually thought I was going be fabulous!' laughs Kate.

'Whenever there's a wedding or a hen night, I'm always first on to the dance flour and I love dancing so I thought I'd be great. Oh, how wrong could you be!

'I rather naively went into it thinking, This is going to be fantastic. I am *so* going to love this. But everyone likes dancing for fun and this is very different. The truth is that I did love it, it *was* fantastic, but I certainly wasn't fabulous.'

Kate's dancing may not have impressed the judges but her resilience and determination won the hearts of the nation, and a lot of votes. Thanks to the public, she kept returning until the judges finally got their way in the week-seven dance off.

'It was fantastic to have that public support,' says the sporting GMTV presenter. 'In a funny sort of way, it added another pressure, although a very welcome one. Even though I had a huge amount of fun, I did take it very seriously and I was very aware that people were spending their money voting me in. To have so many viewers picking up the phone to vote for you is a huge thing. So I really felt like I wanted to pay them back and do well.'

Kate took some hard knocks from the judges, with Craig calling her salsa

'Stumpy, awkward' and Bruno declaring, in week six, 'The nightmare is back!' Nevertheless the popular presenter kept bouncing back.

'I think they were entirely justified,' she says of the comments. 'The great thing about the show is that you have four judges in the studio giving their expert point of view and you have 13 million judges at home with a different point of view.

'You can have someone like Alesha who is obviously fantastically talented and who gets the backing of both and then you have someone like me who is *slightly* less talented (just a little bit) and the viewers might think they deserve another chance.

'That's what makes it so great – because it's not just a black and white decision by four people in the studio. The whole country can get involved.'

As if things weren't bad enough by the middle of the series, calamity Kate was struck with another injury, when she fell in rehearsal and damaged her back. With a strapped up back, she struggled through her final week and was knocked out after scoring 21 for her paso doble.

'If I had any regrets it would be that I went out on another injury because I would have liked to have gone out giving it my best shot,' she said. 'Mind you, I had enough chances so I can't really complain!'

Before she started on the show GMTV colleague Fiona Phillips, who displayed a similar number of left feet in series three, warned Kate that the training was tough.

'Fiona said, "Go for it. You'll have a whale of a time and you'll never be as fit again in your life!" but she also told me it was really, really hard,' she says.

'Of course every year you watch it and see all the videos and hear the celebrities saying how hard it is but you don't really believe it can be that bad. I've run marathons, I've given birth, so I thought to myself, How hard can it be? Then when you actually try it you realize the skill of the people who do it well is incredible. The physical fitness, the ability to think on your feet, literally, is amazing and I take my hat off to all of them.

'I found it physically more demanding than running a marathon although giving birth is slightly more painful – even than dancing with Anton!'

Nonetheless, Kate enjoyed the experience and has continued dancing. She's even about to take ballet lessons.

'That will be a good thing because you have to do that on your own, so you're not taking someone down with you,' she jokes.

'I had the best, best time. Dancing with someone like Anton and being a part of a show like that is just amazing. I know I didn't do well in the eyes of the judges, but I did develop a real love for dancing and I'm glad of that. It's not often in life you try new things, especially as you get older, so it's great to find something new that you love.

'As I said on the show, when I was knocked out, I really hope people will take the plunge and join a dance class because it is huge fun. If even I can enjoy doing it, anyone can.'

Her only problem now is finding a dance partner.

'I struggle to find people to dance with, let's be honest. I can't persuade my husband and Anton probably feels he's already paid his dues!'

The paso doble

The paso is the story of a bullfight so the man is the matador and, originally, the girl was the cape so there are a lot of steps where the girl flows across the floor. The man has strong, dominant lines. In some interpretations the lady is the bull, and she can also have dramatic poses and a more aggressive stance.

What the judges look for:
- Strong and dominant Flamenco movements
- The posture is very important, far more than in any of the other Latin dances. The man should be upright with chest out and bum under
- Like the samba, the paso doble travels round the room
- A flavour of the bullfight — lots of drama, passion and Spanish onions.

Best Couple: Emma Bunton and Darren Bennett got a perfect ten from Bruno and nines from the other three judges in the series-four paso doble, which Bruno called 'grand opera on the dance floor'.

Worst Couple: Dennis Taylor (with Izabela Hannah) and Chris Parker (with Hanna Karttunen) share the lowest score for the paso doble, with 15 each, but you can't beat Chris for sheer entertainment value. His was the funniest paso doble ever seen on the show.

The jive

The dance category is called Latin American but originally it was called Latin and American, and the American bit was the jive. The style goes back to dances like the lindy hop and the jitterbug, and the Swing era when the GIs came over here, and a little bit of rock 'n' roll. All those different forms were mixed together and that became the ballroom jive.

What the judges look for:
- Fast kicks and flicks – a kick comes from the hip and a flick comes from the knee
- Fancy footwork and precise placing
- Fast and energetic movement

Best Couple: Without a doubt **Jill Halfpenny and her partner Darren Bennett** stole the jive crown in series two. Their dance in the final won them a perfect 40. It is still the best jive ever seen on *Strictly*.

Worst Couple: Fiona Phillips and Brendan Cole, who scored 16 in series three.

Austin Healey

Strictly judge Craig Revel Horwood may have met his match in straight-talking Austin Healey. The England rugby star has often created headlines with his views on his team mates, rugby rivals and club managers, and his famously outspoken nature resulted in journalists giving him the nickname 'The Leicester Lip'. But, like our judges, he believes that if something needs to be said, you should say it.

Austin achieved international recognition at an early age, playing for England under 21s in 1992, aged 19. He would also become an integral member of the Leicester team that would dominate the sport from 1998 to 2002. As an all-rounder, he has played in a variety of positions throughout his career – a versatility that could come in handy on the show.

Partner: Erin Boag

During his long stint as a professional, Austin won an impressive 51 caps for England and played in 4 Five/Six Nations tournaments. The low point came when injury prevented him from joining the squad that would go on to win the 2003 World Cup, which he admits was a devastating blow. Retiring in 2006, Austin is now known as a frank and entertaining pundit for both Sky and the BBC.

Austin got his racy name from his granddad, a powerboat racer whose love of all things mechanical led him to suggest it. It was not chosen, as pal Martin Johnson would have it, because he was conceived in the back of an Austin Healey!

Having retired from sport, Austin wanted to take part in *Strictly* because he misses the competitive element. 'I want a challenge and since I've retired nothing has made me nervous or given me a sense of anxiety … until now!' he says. 'The thought of taking part in this has made me petrified! I haven't had that feeling in a long time and it's just the buzz I need.'

He also had a bit of pressure at home, not least from one of his four daughters who said it would be the best thing in the world for her dad to do and even asked whether she was old enough to vote for him.

Austin has been to the *Strictly* studio before, to watch his friend Matt Dawson compete, but he admits he only came because he was hoping he would trip over live on TV or do something really embarrassing.

'The day before Matt's first live show I sent him a barrage of abusive texts trying to unnerve him. Now the boot is on the other foot, I'm leaving my phone at home!'

The 34 year old has no previous dancing experience other than 'being a bit of a hip shaker' when he's on the dance floor with friends. He believed he was quite a good dancer until he started training but he now thinks he's absolutely rubbish.

Brian Fortuna

American **Brian** is set to bring a little Hollywood glitz to the dancers' circle. Having given up competing to concentrate on his stage and television career, he boasts a dancing role in the Leonardo DiCaprio movie *The Aviator* and now lives in showbiz central, Los Angeles.

Born in Philadelphia, the son of top teacher Sandra Fortuna, dancing was in Brian's blood from day one. He was coached at his mother's New Jersey dance school from the age of four and, at five, he began competing.

A specialist in wheelchair ballroom, he performs and teaches for the American DanceWheels Foundation.

As a dancer on the US *Dancing with the Stars* in series four, and a veteran of the live tours, Brian will fit easily into the *Strictly* camp and is looking forward to joining the show. 'I think *Strictly* is going to be the perfect avenue to showcase the activity I have loved since I was a kid,' he says. 'And I'm also really looking forward to spending time enjoying all that England has to offer.'

He'll have the added advantage of being able to understand Vincent, Flavia and Lilia – he speaks fluent Italian and conversational Russian, as well as Spanish, French and Mandarin.

But his ideal celebrity partner would be 'the Queen of England … she's got quite a house!'

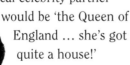

James Jordan

James met wife and dancing partner Aleksandra (known as Ola) in Poland when he auditioned to become her dancing partner in March 2000. Clearly the couple were a perfect match, both on and off the dance floor, and they married in 2003.

Kent-born James began dance classes at 13, encouraged by older sister Kelly, who has since given it up. 'Kelly started at group dance classes,' he says. 'I was pushed into going by my parents. At first I just went along for fun and wasn't really that interested.'

But James quickly impressed his teachers who urged him to compete. By 15, he was a regular at open competitions although he admits that 'at first, I was eliminated very early'.

What kept him going was the girls. 'Suddenly I was doing really well in the competitions. I noticed that girls became more interested in me the more successful I became. It made me try even harder!'

Funding classes with an engineering job, James rose to dizzy heights, becoming a major finalist in all Open International Competitions for Under 21s.

At 21, he decided to take a break from dancing – that is until he heard that Ola was looking for a partner: 'I had seen Ola dance before and thought she was absolutely amazing.' The couple lived in Hong Kong for four years then came back to the UK, where they joined *Strictly* in series four.

In series five, James got along famously with Gabby Logan. The year before, he and Georgina Bouzova seemed to spend more time arguing than they did training.

'I'm patient as long as they listen,' says James.

Speciality: Latin American
Professional Achievements:
North American Top Teacher; North American Amateur Latin Championships;
National Ballroom and Latin Ten Dance Finalist

Speciality: Latin American
Professional Achievements: British Open Rising Star Professional Latin
Runners-Up; UK Open Rising Star Professional Latin American Finalists;
Latin American Closed British Finalists; Professional International Latin
American Championships, ranked Top 12 in World in 2006

Vincent Simone

He may have left series five early with Stephanie Beacham, but **Vincent** is back with all guns blazing. 'I'm going to get my hands on that trophy!' he says confidently.

Vincent and partner Flavia have danced together for 12 years and are world champion Argentine tango experts. They joined *Strictly* in series four when Vincent was paired with *EastEnder* Louisa Lytton.

'I was extremely lucky to be paired up with Louisa as she was probably one of the most talented celebrities to have taken part in the show,' recalls Vincent. 'We had so much fun during the training sessions as I believe that having fun is the best way to learn to dance! She surprised me every Saturday with her performance, always giving it 100 per cent.'

Vincent has years of teaching experience – having started when he was just 12. He began learning at the same time as his parents, in his home town of Foggia, in southern Italy, and was performing by the time he was five. 'I would dance at any party that we went to,' he explains. 'My mother said I was born to perform!' He and his parents, and later his little sister opened a dance school themselves, where Vincent taught.

'I was fairly young to start teaching but I loved it. By the time I was 14, some of the couples I taught were the Italian and Regional Champions. I was so proud of what we had achieved.'

By 16 he was the Italian Youth Champion and at 17 he moved to Surrey and found Flavia.

The cheeky Italian is looking forward to series six, but his celebrity partner may get more than she bargained for. 'I like to joke and am an outrageous flirt – so watch out!'

Speciality: Ten Dance/Argentine tango
Professional Achievements: UK Professional Ten Dance Champions; UK Professional Show Dance Champions; UK Argentine Tango Show Champions; World Argentine Tango Show Champions; World and European Ten Dance and Showdance Finalist

Ian Waite

Ian joined *Strictly Come Dancing* in series two, and made an immediate impact with Denise Lewis. The elegant pair came second and then repeated the same feat in the Champion of Champions show. He followed the success with Zoe Ball, in series three.

'I was the luckiest man being paired with Zoe,' he says. 'She was amazing and we formed a great partnership. Zoe won so many of the shows in terms of the judges' marks. I feel that's an achievement in itself.'

Growing up in Reading, Ian was more interested in rugby, football and tennis but when his dad began dancing he dragged his two boys along to his Saturday-morning class. Ian refused to set foot on the dance floor but the girls were soon sick of him standing on the sidelines and dragged him up. He was hooked!

At 13, Ian entered the open competition circuit, where he achieved considerable success in the Youth arena, becoming European Youth Latin American Champion. He lived in Holland for four years and in 1997 became the Dutch Professional Champion. However, a split with his Dutch partner meant he was close to giving up. Four years ago, he teamed up with Camilla Dallerup.

'The best thing about dancing is the thrill of performing,' he says. 'Performing is my thing – I'm a bit of a show off!'

Speciality: Latin American
Professional Achievements: Dutch Professional Champion; French Open Professional Runner-up; Open British Professional Rising Stars Runner-up; European Professional Latin American Finalist; World Professional Showdance Finalist; World Masters Professional Latin American Finalist; UK Closed Professional Latin American Runner-up; World Professional Latin American Showdance Runner-up

Len Goodman

Head judge Len Goodman has been kept on his toes for the last year with the fifth series of *Strictly* as well as two series of *Dancing with the Stars* in the States. With one of the US seasons clashing with the British show, that meant a lot of air miles.

'During series five, I was flying to Los Angeles and back once a week,' reveals Len. 'The flying is fine, but the eight-hour time difference does affect you. I've found it's best not to try to overcome the jet lag so if I were tired at midday, I'd go to bed. Then I'd be wide awake at night so I'd get up and read a book, and I'd go to bed again at three in the morning. I had to be ready to perform for the show on Saturday nights, because you can't sit there yawning your head off.'

Luckily, there was nothing to induce a yawn in the dancers' performances this year, with a hotbed of talent vying for the judges' votes.

'From week one there were some really strong dancers,' remembers Len. 'The celebrities do the show for different reasons but once they get going they get very competitive and take it really seriously. They don't want to let their professionals down. As much as the celebrities want to do well, ballroom dancing is very competitive so the professionals all want to beat each other.'

The girls got off to a particularly strong start. For the first time ever three couples scored in the thirties for their initial dance, with a record score of 36 for Alesha Dixon and Matthew Cutler. But Len is a strong believer that it's not where you start, it's where you finish.

'It's not a bad thing to start slow because then you have room to grow. As much as the judges try to judge fairly on each week's performance, you can't help having a few preconceived ideas – if somebody comes out in week one and dances fantastically and you give them a nine, your expectations for the following week are high.

If somebody is terrible in week one, any slight improvement is encouraging.

'It is very difficult to start well and then maintain it. Kelly and Alesha both began beautifully but then Kelly and Brendan broke the rules by putting three lifts in the American smooth so we had to mark them down. Then Kelly did the paso doble and took over the role of matador, which I hated.'

In fact Len, who is not usually one for regrets, wishes he'd been kinder to Kelly.

'I was terribly sorry that Kelly had to leave. I think she had the potential to go much further,' he says. 'What made it worse for me was the last week she danced I was quite harsh towards her. They performed the samba and it wasn't up to her standard. I moaned that she had more talent than Brendan showed.

'I was trying to gee them up to come back stronger but I didn't know that she'd had a terrible week and her dad was in hospital. Then she left the series, so the last memory she'll have of me is moaning about their performances.'

Avid viewers of the series will know that Len has often been frustrated when good dancers are voted off. To combat this, the dance off was introduced in series five, whereby the two couples with the lowest scores dance again to keep their place in the show.

'The dance off was introduced because in the series before DJ Spooney and Ray Fearon were voted off too early. We wanted to make it into more of a dance competition and less of a popularity contest, but it didn't always happen. We ended up with a situation where Penny and Gabby, who were both good, were in the dance off.

'There are some bizarre decisions. How could Kenny Logan go further than Gabby Logan, for instance? How could Kate stay when Penny went? It's crazy but that's part of the charm of the show. The viewers have their say just as we do.'

As a former ballroom champion, with 30 years' experience of running a dance school, Len knows exactly what he's looking for in a performance. As head judge it fell to him to choose who left the show in the event of a tie. It's a responsibility he takes in his stride.

'It is a doddle if all three of the others agree,' he laughs. 'Two or three times I had to decide who should go, but Gabby and Penny was definitely the most difficult.'

Despite his tendency to lose his temper with his fellow judges, Len is always supportive of the celebrity dancers.

'It's a gruelling three months. I admire all the celebrities for having the guts to have a go at something they don't really know they'll be any good at,' he says. 'That's why I can't be ultra-nasty. What's wonderful about *Strictly* is you are watching people who can't dance and then suddenly they get it.'

As series six approaches, Len is looking forward to sitting at the head of the judges' panel once more and he's still a big fan of the show. 'With live bands, great singers, fabulous dancing, Bruce with his corny jokes, the judges to boo at, it's a little bit of pantomime,' he says. 'It's not like other shows where contestants have their hearts set on being singers and then are told they're useless. Mark Ramprakash doesn't want to be a dancer: he's a cricketer. Once they're kicked off, they go back to what they're very good at, so it's harmless entertainment.'

Bruno's Breakdown

This year, *Strictly*'s most florid judge, Bruno Tonioli, will be appearing on the show in three countries, at almost the same time! Before the start of series six, however, he was taking a well-earned break.

'I'm doing the series in Australia, then America, then the UK,' he says. 'It's going to be quite insane. I can only do the beginning of the run in Australia, because there is no time to carry on. Then I will do the US and the UK at the same time. It's surreal, so I've taken some time off to charge my batteries.'

In series five, Bruno proved his judging credentials when he singled out Alesha and Kelly as the two best dancers in the group Swing.

'The men should be afraid, very afraid, because these girls mean business,' he said. 'How to pick a jewel from all these wonderful girls ... but, I would say, the two hot brunettes – Alesha and Kelly. I can't wait to come back.'

Of course, Alesha went on to win and Kelly's dancing was consistently impressive, before her early exit due to bereavement in week eight. And while he believes the right couples reached the final, he says the dance off caused a few upsets along the away.

'The dance off was a great idea but because of the way the votes came back from the public, it created the worst-possible scenario,' he recalls. 'The least popular person with the judges was not always in the dance off. That was the biggest surprise in the series and it happened quite a few times.'

Biggest Shock

Gabby and Penny – the battle of the legs! The big controversy of the season! Both surprised me and, despite all the controversy, it was the public who kicked them out. They both really exceeded my expectations and should have stayed longer.

Kate Garraway

I absolutely love her! Her attitude was great. She should have gone way before she did, but it's the nation's show and if the public want to see people then that's their prerogative. In the last season I think people began to feel a little bit high and mighty and disagreed with us, and then we ended up with this strange dance off. We do disagree but, overall, the judges' scores are pretty fair. It doesn't bother me though. I understand that a lot of *Strictly*'s appeal is seeing somebody you like – and getting her back to see how ridiculous she will be next week. The good thing about Kate is that she laughed with us. She really did put the work in. It was a bit of a replay of Fiona Phillips two years before. There is something about GMTV that precludes you from being a good dancer. Talk about the best of the worst!

Most Impressive Dance

Kelly and Brendan's American smooth. The scores were robbed from Kelly. I gave her a ten when everybody else penalized her for the illegal lifts as it wasn't her fault; it was Brendan's. That was a beautiful, stunning dance. I know the rules but I had to make something clear – so they gave her eight, I gave her ten. I thought that dance was wonderful. She could easily have been in the final. It was a bit of a scandal, but that was my personal reaction. Give her a nine, OK, but an eight? It was the best dance to date – it was stunning.

Best Dancer

Alesha Dixon was great and deserved to win. It was incredible because I thought the Latin would be her strength but in fact she was magic in ballroom. You don't expect a sassy, sexy girl to do it so well. She did a fantastic job, and I was so happy she won.

Most Improved

Matt Di Angelo improved so much. We had a bit of a shaky start and then we had terrible problems in the quarter-finals and we thought he was going to get kicked out. That challenged the foregone conclusion that he was going to be in the final, but he did apply himself and he got to the final, which is a great achievement. The great thing about the show is the improvement; even Kate, bless her, got a bit better! It's tough because you're up against Alesha, Kelly, Penny etc., but even she, in her own kind of dancing madness, improved. She started to be almost decent.

Other Surprises

Gethin Jones became kind of sexy, suddenly. He's a very handsome guy but he didn't act very well, especially in the sexy, smouldering Latin stuff. He suddenly got it one week after we had a go at him about it. He unleashed the beast and let the dragon out. Letitia really was great in the end. The series was two weeks longer than the year before and the more you do something, the better you get. Everybody improved by the later stages.

Best Dancer Overall

I think each series' winner has their own qualities. Alesha's win was very deserved as she's a great all-rounder. But I think I would have to put Darren Gough and Jill Halfpenny in the mix. Jill is still the best jiver to date and Darren's quickstep is the most unexpected talent. He was just remarkable. He made me smile, which is what the show's all about.

To John Barnes on his salsa:
'The hip action! Have you got a ferret down your pants?'

On Willie Thorne's tango:
He looks so uncomfortable – like a polar bear in the Sahara.'

On Matt's tango
'You're strong and proud. You're like a snarling young lion at times.'

On Letitia's jive to Meatloaf's 'Deadringer':
'Instead of a Dead Ringer it was a lookey likey of a jive.'

On Gethin's cha-cha-cha:
'It was like the action man running out of steam.'

On Gethin's salsa:
'Full Thrust ahead – you're turning into the loin king!'

Lisa Snowdon

Her best pal is David Walliams and her ex is George Clooney, so it seems Lisa Snowdon loves a ladies' man. She should get on like a house on fire with dance partner Brendan Cole!

The model and TV presenter started life in Welwyn Garden City but moved to London at a young age to study at the Italia Conti School of Performing Arts. At 19, she was spotted by a model scout in a nightclub, and after a photographer friend suggested she try and get a bigger agency, she joined Premier Model Management, where she has been ever since.

Lisa's career has seen her model in photo shoots for likes of *Vogue*, *Marie Claire* and *Cosmopolitan*, and front advertising campaigns for big brands including Mercedes-Benz, Martini, Lynx, Gossard and Fabergé. Her appearance in a Kellogg's Special K commercial caught the eye of TV executives and Lisa was offered a job presenting on MTV. Having proved she's more than a pretty face, she now works regularly as a presenter in both the US and the UK. Lisa has two sisters, Lesley-Anne and Joanna.

Partner: Brendan Cole

The 36 year old jumped at the chance to compete on her favourite TV show. 'It's the best show on television and I love watching it. So do my two sisters and my nan,' she says. 'I will never miss an episode – it's everyone's dream to be involved in *Strictly* and I am so excited about it and honoured to be involved.' She particularly loved the last series and thought Matt and Gethin were fantastic and Alesha was just beautiful, but she's hoping the competition isn't quite so tough this time around.

Although she did a little dancing at stage school, Lisa says she is prepared for any criticism the judges throw at her. 'Being a model you get used to rejection and criticism – you just learn to get a thick skin,' she explains. 'But I will put my heart and soul into this and I'm sure I'll get disheartened if I get criticized but I will take it on board and listen.'

Lisa has a close family and is determined to make them proud, as well as making Brendan proud. 'I want to take as much from this experience as I can. I may start getting competitive at a later date but at the moment I'm just getting excited and at the same time apprehensive.

'My goal is to get praise from at least one of the judges, from Brendan and from my family. My family are very honest with me, and if it was rubbish, they'd tell me!'

Strictly Awards

Most hours trained

Alesha Dixon and Matthew Cutler trained for 401 hours in series five, which is over 30 hours per week. This incredible achievement makes the previous record-holders, Mark Ramprakash and Karen Hardy, look like slackers – with 312.5 hours. In total, the couples in series five trained for 2865.7 hours.

Most stroppy professional

Anton du Beke was uncharacteristically spiky with the judges throughout series five, exploding on several occasions after their unkind comments on Kate's dancing. 'It was nonsense,' he spouted after another mauling for her paso doble. 'I don't know what they're talking about!' Later he told her, 'You were as good as any of them and it really gives me the hump.'

Best at dancing through the pain

Bill Turnbull in series three, who battled through a swollen ankle and nasty rash, has a serious contender for his crown in Kate Garraway. Beginning the show with two strapped ankles and ending, in week seven, with her back strapped up, she battled through and refused to give up, despite a considerable amount of pain.

Most dignified exit

Stephanie Beacham showed characteristic class when she was the first female celebrity to be voted off. 'Oh, thank goodness,' she said, to laughter and applause. 'It's been nothing but awful. I have adored watching the hard work – watching it with cups in my hand – I am in such admiration for these glorious dancers. How they do it I do not know. I am so grateful to be let out of my misery.'

Most appropriate song

After **Kate** hurt her back in the week of the paso, she and Anton danced to the song 'Somebody Told Me'. The first line is, 'Breaking my back just to know your name …' And the band? The Killers.

Most impressive lift

What **Kenny Logan** lacked in style he made up for in brute strength. As well as nabbing the sought-after *Dirty Dancing* lift in the group number, he managed *Strictly*'s first one-armed lift in his show eight American smooth. Bruno was impressed, saying, 'What a monumental effort, and what a tower of strength.' Len, however, was not so keen, 'It's not *Strictly Come Weightlifting*,' he grouched.

Gary Rhodes OBE

Celebrity chef Gary Rhodes will be cooking up a storm on the dance floor and hopes to come up with a tasty tango and a spicy salsa.
'I love the beauty and glamour of ballroom, but I enjoy the faster pace of Latin,' he reveals. 'Now I'm training, it's a question of juggling the two. I do love the "top hat and tails" for the ballroom though…'

Born and bred in Kent, Gary's love of food began as a youngster when he helped his mum out by cooking for his sisters. His kitchen experiments led him to a catering course at Thanet Technical College in Kent where he not only found the passion to make him one of Britain's top chefs but also fell in love with future wife, Jennie.

Partner: Karen Hardy

From there he went from strength to strength, becoming a big name in the business and landing himself four Michelin stars. At 27, he made his first television appearance on *Hot Chefs,* where his spiky hair, energetic nature and down-to-earth approach made him an instant hit. He soon had his own TV shows, fronting the enormously popular *Rhodes Around Britain, Masterchef,* and *Hell's Kitchen* and, as well as running his successful restaurants, he has found time to write 18 cookery books.

Gary and Jennie, who have two sons, have watched the show for years and they are hoping this will lead to a new hobby for both of them.

'Each time I've been watching I've been wishing I could dance like that – and my wife has also been wishing I could dance like that. I'm very proud (and very scared) to be taking part.

'I hope this leads on to a great social pastime for my wife and me to enjoy together for many years to come.'

Gary, who last danced in a club several years ago, has no experience of ballroom and Latin at all and says he is very much 'starting from scratch'. But dance partner Karen Hardy won't have any trouble getting Gary to work his socks off, as he reckons he is a workaholic. A normal day starts at 4.30 a.m. with 250 stomach crunches in his home gym and he is rarely home from work before 10 p.m.

'I think I've got the best teacher in Karen,' he says. 'She's a brilliant dancer and a World Champion, so I couldn't be in better hands.'

Viewers of *Hell's Kitchen* will know that as well as being passionate Gary can also be very competitive. When asked if he has his eye on the top prize he says, simply, 'Who *doesn't* want to win!?'

The Ballroom Dances

The Argentine tango

The Argentine tango is said to be the story of a gaucho, who's been riding his horse across the Pampas and who rides into town, goes into a bar and finds an attractive lady of the night. It's a courtship, but a little raunchier, so the hold is much closer and tighter than in any other ballroom dance. The lady's left hand is lower because she is supposed to be checking for a wallet in his back pocket!

What the judges look for:
- Passion and drama, good storytelling
- Very clever, intricate foot work and leg work, with kicks and flicks between each other's legs, dragging and jumping
- Strong lines formed by the legs
- Tight hold

Best Couple: Series-four winners **Mark Ramprakash and Karen Hardy** hadn't had a single ten by the time they reach the semi-final. Their dramatic Argentine tango gained them three tens, and a total score of 39.

Worst Couple: The Argentine tango has only been danced since series four and is performed in the semi-finals, meaning that only six couples have attempted it so far. **Matt Dawson and Lilia Kopylova** have the lowest score with 30, for a dance that Craig dismissed as 'dreary'.

The ballroom tango

Many years ago, the tango was a Latin dance and the jive was a ballroom dance. But the jive was the only ballroom dance that was taken out of hold while the tango was the only Latin that wasn't free, so they changed over. But the hold is much tighter than the normal ballroom dances and it's an aggressive dance, rather than an elegant one.

A frequent criticism on the show is that the dancers put too much Argentine in the ballroom. The Argentine has more scope for fun and clever moves like the leg flicks, but the ballroom tango should be staccato. There's a sharpness about it and that's where it differs.

What the judges look for:
- A fixed, more regimented hold
- Sharp, staccato actions. The girl's head is predominantly to the left but when they go side by side, which is called promenade position, her head moves from left to right, which is when you see the sharp head movements
- Flexed knees, in a stalking movement, and sharp, jabbing feet
- Drama, aggression

Best Couple: Zoe Ball and Ian Waite performed the tango twice in series three, getting 38 points on both occasions. 'Drop dead gorgeous,' declared an enraptured Bruno. **Alesha Dixon and Matthew Cutler** achieved a similar response and score for their week-nine tango in series five. Arlene named Alesha the 'tantalizing tango temptress'.

Worst Couple: Diarmuid Gavin and Nicole Cutler scored 13 points for a dance that was, according to Craig, 'painful to watch'.

The quickstep

It's bright; it's lively. In all ballroom, with the exception of the Argentine tango, the three keys are hold, posture and movement. The quickstep is like moving across hot coals, but without making it look hectic. It's not fast and furious. Just like the garden talked about earlier, there should be a balance of lawn and flowers with the quickstep too.

What the judges look for:
- A good balance between fast steps and elegant movement
- Feet that look light on the floor, giving the impression that they hardly make contact at all
- Skipping, tripping and running smoothly across the floor
- Good hold
- Beautiful posture

Best Couple: Colin Jackson and Erin Boag's quickstep in the final of series three was the perfect example of a light and elegant ballroom dance and scored 39 from the judges.

Worst Couple: Diarmuid Gavin and Nicole Cutler's chaotic quickstep in series two prompted Len to say; 'The quickstep is like a soufflé. It's light and fluffy. This was more like a spotted dick!' They scored 12.

The waltz

The waltz is the oldest of all the ballroom dances. The slow version is actually the English waltz, because before that, in the eighteenth century, came the Viennese waltz, but that is so hectic and exhausting that people couldn't keep that up all night long. Instead, they took the same steps, with three beats to the bar, and produced a slower dance.

What the judges look for:
- Classic ballroom hold: the woman slightly to the man's right with her left hand on his upper arm and his right hand on her shoulder blade
- Rise and fall through the legs
- Elegance

The Mother of Strictly

Still going strong as it enters its sixth season, *Strictly* still has some way to go to catch up with its predecessor, *Come Dancing*. The show, which saw dancers competing in teams, ran from 1949 to 1995, making it the longest-running TV show at the time.

Come Dancing was conceived by impresario Eric Morley as a way to bring the joys of dancing to the public at large. First broadcast from the Manchester Ritz Ballroom on 29 September 1949, it concentrated initially on teaching the moves, with professional dancers Syd Perkins and Edna Duffield taking the public through their paces while MacDonald Hobley hosted.

In 1953, the format was changed to make it a dance competition with regional heats, where teams competed in various style sections and were awarded points by the judges. Winners went through and the series culminated in a national final. Broadcast live from ballrooms around the country, it proved a smash hit.

Keith Jones, the development director at Mecca Leisure, worked closely with Eric Morley on the programme for 21 years.

'In the days of *Come Dancing*, we were dealing with a different public,' Keith says. 'They had ballrooms in every town and everybody danced, going right back to 1912 when the foxtrot started and dancing together became all the rage. Even then the old guard said it was "indecent" because the dancers put their arms around each other. Of course, that only served to make it even more popular.

'It all went from there and right up to the war; all ages danced the same. When young people learned the waltz it was the same waltz as someone who was 60 was dancing. That's all changed. Kids go to clubs or learn street dancing and their parents dance in a different style, but when *Come Dancing* started it appealed to young people as well as older people.'

Keith has recently retired from the position of Vice President of the British Dance Council after 18 years, and is now Life Vice President.

'Eric Morley came up with the idea and it proved incredibly popular,' he recalls. 'Eric was Vice President before me and he was part of the academic scene of dancing although, funnily enough, he wasn't a dancer. But then you don't have to be Lewis Hamilton to be an enthusiast of Formula One!'

Despite its popularity, the early years of *Come Dancing* lacked something of the glitz, glamour and garish colour associated with ballroom – it was broadcast in black and white.

'In those days, if you saw the show in person you would say, "Who the hell chose these colours?"' says Keith, who served as a judge on many occasions. 'They wore dreadful colours but black and white really meant different shades of grey, so if you took a certain blue, a certain red and a certain green, they could look exactly the same on screen. We would see a girl in a riot of colour, with orange, blue and all sorts we'd think, Good God! But on screen, it looked very different.

'They used to tell us to wear pale, blue shirts rather than white, because the lighting would reflect on white and you get a ghost line round your lapel.'

Over the years the show was presented by a string of famous faces including Peter West, Angela Rippon, Michael Aspel, Judith Chalmers, Noel Edmonds and finally Rosemarie Ford.

Surprisingly, it was never fronted by our own twinkle-toed host Brucie, although he did appear on one show.

'Rosemarie Ford, who had done *The Generation Game* with me, was the host in the 1990s,' he explains. 'Because we'd danced quite a bit in the *The Generation Game*, she asked me if I would consider doing a quickstep with her. I went down to Bournemouth to the ballroom there and I was one of the professional dancers in a little exhibition. But I never hosted the show. I was too young then!'

Nonetheless, Bruce was a big fan. 'I always liked the series and when my darling wife, Wilnelia, first came over to this country she loved it. She adored the dresses and the dancing and was a huge fan, and I always said it shouldn't have come off when it did.

'Mind you, it was probably a good thing because it made *Strictly Come Dancing* so new and, with the reworked format for today's audience, it is now a different show altogether.'

Head judge Len Goodman also has fond memories of the show, on which he appeared as both a dancer and a judge.

'I danced the cha-cha-cha on it for Home Counties South, in around 1969, but sadly there's no film of it,' he says. 'We had to go to a Mecca ballroom called the Orchid, in Purley, near Croydon, and it was my first television appearance ever. It was

nerve-racking because I'd only been dancing two years and, suddenly, there I was on the television with my mum watching. It was very exciting.

'Later on, I judged it a few times. They were very fuddy-duddy and they told me I had to wear a white dinner jacket, but I didn't have one so they got me one, which was about two sizes too big.

'I remember we had to keep our comments very, very short and very

positive. We couldn't say anything negative. I judged a bizarre section that they called "Off Beat", which was like disco dancing, or anything that wasn't Latin or Ballroom. The standard was awful!

'We still had to find positive things to say but that's how I've always judged. On *Strictly,* I always try to come up with a positive before I go into the negative comments.'

Such was the difference in the standards of the competitors, however, that Keith Jones admits there was sometimes a little massaging of the scores.

'The dancers were grouped into areas, and, of course, the standard could depend on the population of the region,' he reveals.

'If you have a team from Birmingham or Manchester, they have more dancers to chose from than somewhere like East Anglia. So East Anglia had a very poor team while South London, under Peggy Spencer, had a very posh team. Some ballrooms had better reputations for dancing than others, so the difference in quality between the teams was always a bit of a problem.

'We used to arrange the marks a little – but not fiddle them. For example, if you thought South London was worth 5 for each dance and East Anglia was only worth 1, then the overall score would end up at 100 versus 10. Then you were in danger of upsetting people so much that they wouldn't enter again, so we had to keep the scores close. The wrong team never won, but the difference was manipulated so that, if the two teams were worth 5 and 1, we'd give them 5 and 3, to lower the gap between top and bottom.'

Just as well the judges on *Strictly* have no such qualms!

John Sergeant

John Sergeant has dodged bullets in war zones, tackled evasive politicians in hard-hitting interviews and even sparred with Paul Merton and Ian Hislop on *Have I Got News for You.* But for the 64-year-old journalist, *Strictly* could still prove one of his biggest challenges.

With no experience of dance, he can't even remember the last time he attempted it. 'Probably a hundred years ago!' he laughs. 'I think it was some time last century!'

John's father, a vicar, had been keen for him to learn ballroom as a lad and had sent him to a few lessons, but John admits he was more interested in chatting up the girls.

Although he has been a heavyweight political journalist for forty years, John is no stranger to light entertainment, appearing, in recent years, on *Have I Got News For You, Room 101* and *QI.* In fact, after leaving university in 1966, John declined a news trainee position with Reuters for the opportunity to appear in Alan Bennett's award-winning BBC comedy series *On the Margin*.

Partner: Kristina Rihanoff

Returning to his first career choice, John worked on the *Liverpool Echo* for three years before landing a position at the BBC, where he worked his way up to become one of the most respected political pundits in the business.

John believes he has Margaret Thatcher to thank for one of his career highlights. In 1990, he was reporting from outside the British Embassy in Paris where he proclaimed to 13 million TV viewers that Mrs Thatcher would not be coming out of the Embassy to make a statement about her recent leadership ballot – while behind him she was doing just that! This clip won him a British Press Guild Award for most memorable TV moment of the year. In 2000, John switched to ITN to become their political editor.

John's wife, Mary, who has rarely seen her husband dance during their 40-year marriage, is a huge fan of the programme, but reckons he will be absolutely hopeless!

'When I was approached to take part I thought the idea was absurd,' admits John. 'Then I decided it was about time I did something a bit absurd!'

He is looking forward to making all his colleagues back in the news room incredibly jealous by dancing with his stunning dance partner, Kristina.

A veteran *Strictly* viewer, John particularly enjoyed watching Natasha Kaplinsky in series one and reveals that Tony Benn voted for her five times!

John doesn't have his sights set on the trophy, mainly because, he says, 'I don't have a hope in hell!' His main ambition is not to look like an idiot, and to inspire the older generation to try a few dance lessons themselves. 'I'm hoping to get the sympathy vote, the over-60 vote and the underdog vote!'

Hayley Holt

Hayley may be new to the UK audience but she is no stranger to the format, having danced on three seasons of the New Zealand show, *Dancing with the Stars*.

And she'll be meeting up with some familiar faces backstage – as Brendan Cole and Craig Revel Horwood are judges on the programme. Hayley first started dancing at the age of seven, when she went to keep a friend company. She remembers that 'my brother Logan and I used to call it "boring dancing".' Both soon changed their minds and Logan became her dance partner for competitions, meaning the family had every weekend taken up with dancing. 'My whole extended family used to come along,' laughs Hayley. 'It was their weekly social event!'

After ten years on the amateur circuit Hayley turned professional at 17. 'I felt I had outgrown the New Zealand amateur competition but didn't want to move overseas.'

Although great success followed, with Hayley and her partner being placed eighteenth in the Professional Rising Star at Blackpool and sixth at the US Open before winning the National Championships at home, Hayley decided her future was in her other passion: snowboarding! Thanks to stints on *Dancing with the Stars* and other New Zealand shows, however, the 28 year old didn't hang up her dancing shoes entirely.

Having coached the last male celebrity to leave in two series of *Dancing with the Stars*, Hayley is looking forward to her new challenge. 'I am excited, nervous and a bit overwhelmed, and I am chomping at the bit to get started!'

> **Speciality:** Ballroom
> **Professional Achievements**
> New Zealand Professional Ballroom Champion; US Open Professional Ballroom Rising Star Finalist; Blackpool Professional Ballroom Rising Star Quarter Finalist

Ola Jordan

Polish Latin American champ **Ola** danced with Gabby's husband Kenny Logan in series five and managed to get him through to the final five, despite some clunky routines.

'Kenny wasn't the best dancer but he was a lovely person – he really made the show for me,' says Ola. 'I enjoyed every minute. Without sounding cruel, I can teach anyone after Kenny!'

Husband James had better watch out. Her ideal celeb partner is Robbie Williams and she is hoping for 'someone young and good-looking, who's a sweet person, or else someone who can dance and will get me to the final!'

Ola was born and bred in a small town called Legionowo, near Warsaw. She started dancing at the age of 12, after lessons were advertised at school.

Her tutors were so impressed that they encouraged her to enrol in a proper dance class where she could practise with a permanent partner and compete. Within six months of her first dance lesson Ola was entering competitions.

After years of earning various 'classes' – the equivalent of medals – she took part in the Youth Closed Polish Championships and she won first place. In 1999, at the age of 17, she won the Open Polish Championship, and the same year went to the World Championships where she was placed in the Top 12.

After the championship, Ola was in the market for a new partner when James called and asked if he could try out.

Although they are a perfect couple off the dance floor, *Strictly Come Dancing* brings out the competitive streak.

'There is a bit of competition between us of course, but we both want each other to do the best we can,' she says. 'But I do want to win!'

> **Speciality:** Latin American
> **Professional Achievements:** British Open Rising Star Professional Latin Runners-Up; UK Open Rising Star Professional Latin American Finalists; Latin American Closed British Finalists; Professional International Latin American Championships, ranked Top 12 in World in 2006

Lilia Kopylova

Russian doll **Lilia** has many strings to her dancing bow. She specializes in Latin American but also trained in ballet and gymnastics, and started ice-skating aged four, becoming a Moscow figure-skating champ.

Lilia didn't start dance training until she was nine because the close contact involved was frowned upon by the strict authorities in Russia at that time. Instead, she watched all the dancing she could on television.

After her grandmother signed her up for ballroom lessons, however, Lilia was hooked. At 15, she and dance partner were Russian Ten Dance Champions and she decided it was time to choose between the Latin and ballroom.

'I chose the Latin because you can express yourself more. I still enjoy teaching it [ballroom] but don't choose to dance it competitively.'

Lilia's family moved from Russia to Denmark and later to England. Her parents supported her as she pursued her passion in all three places.

With Darren her career reached new heights and their most treasured memory is competing as part of the UK team at the Open British Championships in Blackpool in 2004, their first major contest as professionals. Working with her husband every day does mean the occasional row, she admits, but it's soon forgotten in the dance.

'We have two lives – professional and private,' says Lilia. 'We may fight on the floor, but when we leave the dancing hall everything is behind us – it's gone, it's forgotten.'

Lilia has been paired with Aled Jones, Matt Dawson and Dominic Littlewood. Her greatest success to date, however, is taking the series-three trophy, and the Christmas special prize, with cricketer Darren Gough.

'Darren was great to work with. He's so easy to teach and we had really fun sessions but worked incredibly hard.'

Speciality: Latin American
Professional Achievements: UK Closed Professional Latin Champions; British National Professional Latin Champions; World Professional Latin Finalists; British Show Dance Champions; World Professional Rising Star Champions

Kristina Rihanoff

Stunning Siberian **Kristina** may be a novice in the ways of *Strictly Come Dancing* but won't have any problem with the tutoring side of things – she has been teaching since she was 16.

'You need to find a way to make it simple for them, while having fun,' she says. 'Then, even when the work gets hard, they still feel like they are having a good time.'

Kristina's love of dance began with childhood ballet classes. She then trained in Latin and Standard styles, Rhythm and Theatre Arts but found that it was the Latin harmonies that stirred her passion.

Competing from the age of seven, Kristina became a renowned dance champion in Siberia but never neglected her studies, gaining a master's degree in tourism and hospitality.

In 2001, she moved to Seattle, Washington, to compete and three years later represented the US at the Blackpool Dance Festival, where she came second in the Theatre Dance category. Soon afterwards, Kristina returned to her Latin roots with a new partner and won the South African Championship.

Kristina's favourite Latin dance is the rumba, 'that is the woman's dance. As it is so slow, it allows the lady to be very sensual and beautiful. The rumba really shows off the leg action and footwork.'

'*Strictly Come Dancing* is a marvellous show,' she says. 'My hope is to perform routines that are unique, entertaining, and exciting.'

And, if she gets knocked out, she can help out backstage. Her hobby is professional make-up and she has even written a book about it!

Speciality: Latin American/mambo
Professional Achievements: British Open Latin Semi-Finalist; US National American Rhythm Finalist; South African International Latin Champion; British World Exhibition Finalist; Mambo Open Championship Finalist; Rising Star US Champions – American Rhythm

Let's Face the Music

Live music is an integral part of the magic of *Strictly Come Dancing* but turning a modern pop song into the perfect paso doble is little short of a musical miracle. The daunting task of producing 90-second arrangements for all the dances, with less than a week's notice, falls to Musical Director David Arch.

'Sometimes it's difficult to squeeze it down but some songs are harder than others,' says David. 'The dancers often have ideas about which bits must be kept in, so they can choreograph certain sections, and that makes it more difficult. There's a lot of toing and froing and the arrangement has to be approved all round.

'All this has to be done in a week – I wish it were more. Occasionally, things are put in place on the Friday, giving me eight days, but obviously nothing can be decided until the result of the show, so it's all a very quick turn-round.'

David took over from Laurie Holloway in series four and, before that, had a wide and varied career in film, television and pop. As well as playing on the soundtrack of *Notting Hill*, *The Golden Compass* and three Harry Potter films, he has been musical director on *Strictly Dance Fever* and *Just the Two of Us*. He has also worked with musical stars as diverse as Leona Lewis, Andrea Bocelli and Robbie Williams.

Although he admits he's no expert in ballroom and Latin ('I'm just a musician') he took the show very much in his stride.

'It's all live telly and not much rehearsal. You never get used to working under pressure but I knew what to expect.'

The incredibly wide range of styles required for the programme means versatility is essential. Songs range from the classic, such as 'You're the Tops' and 'Putting on the Ritz', to the ultra-modern, such as Franz Ferdinand's 'Take Me Out' and Jack Johnson's 'Better When We're Together'.

On the night, the songs are played by the 15 musicians who make up the *Strictly* band and sung by

lead singer Tommy Blaze and three other vocalists, Hayley Sanderson, Lance Ellington and Priscilla Jones.

Amazingly, the band don't get together to rehearse until the afternoon of the live Saturday show.

'The rehearsals for the band are so quick that, by the time we are live on air, we're probably playing it for the third or fourth time,' reveals David. 'I've spent all week writing it all out and then I turn up on the Saturday and the first time we play it, the couples are dancing to it.'

'The music is chosen between the production team and the dancers,' he says. 'They all sign them off and give them to me. A couple of times we've had to say, "no, we can't do that" because it's for a full orchestra. Where you've got to play it live with 15 instruments, it doesn't really work.

'The hardest for us are the dramatic dances, like the

The Ballroom Dances

The American smooth

In America, where they can't stand anything elegant, they invented another branch of dancing, which they called the American smooth. Basically you can dance the waltz, the Viennese waltz or the foxtrot as the American smooth and most people choose the latter. The difference is that you're allowed to break the hold. It goes back to the old Hollywood musicals, the Fred and Ginger-style dances, and that's the flavour of the smooth. The ruling on the show is that you must be in hold for 40 per cent of the dance, and that is a good rule because otherwise it becomes a show dance.

What the judges look for:
- A seamless transition from hold to release and then back to hold
- Fluid movements
- Erect and elegant posture, in and out of hold
- At least 40 per cent in hold
- A maximum of two lifts

Best Couple: Darren Gough and Lilia Kopylova managed a perfect score for the American smooth in the 2007 Christmas special. Within the main series, **Colin Jackson and Erin Boag** received a score of 37 and a perfect ten from Arlene who said, 'You put the fizz into physical'. Kelly Brook and Brendan Cole danced a show-stopping American smooth in series five but were penalized for adding an extra lift, ending up with one ten, from Bruno, and a total score of 34.

Worst Couple: John Barnes and Nicole Cutler scored just 22 in series five for a dance that Craig called 'dull'.

The foxtrot

If you ask professional dancers which ballroom dance they like the best, most will say the foxtrot, because it is the most elegant of all the dances. Invented by vaudeville performer Harry Fox, it's a simple style with a lot of walking but its simplicity makes it very difficult to do well. It's an elegant, smooth, gliding dance with the timing varying between slow and fast.

What the judges look for:
- A dance that glides across the floor
- Gentle rise and fall, not as pronounced as in the waltz. It should be like a calm ocean with a slight ripple
- Walks and chassés
- Constant, flowing movement
- Classic ballroom hold
- Elegant posture

Best Couple: Darren Gough and Lilia Kopylova scored 36 for their foxtrot in the series-three final, including a perfect ten from Len, who said Darren was 'surprisingly light on his feet'.

Worst Couple: Fiona Phillips and Brendan Cole once more failed to impress the judges with their week-four foxtrot, which scored 20 and got them voted off.

Don Warrington MBE

Don Warrington is swapping *Rising Damp* for rise and fall when he joins *Strictly Come Dancing* in series six. The actor has held a place in the nation's heart since he first sprang to fame as Rigsby's cultured tenant, Philip Smith, in the long-running seventies' TV sitcom, which also starred Leonard Rossiter and Richard Beckinsale and Frances de la Tour.

The classic thespian, who has performed at the National Theatre, Bristol Old Vic and with the English Shakespeare Company, is bemused by the reputation the cult show left him with. 'It always comes as a surprise to me that I'm thought of as a comic actor,' he admits. 'Because I don't think I'm terribly funny at all.'

Partner: Lilia Kopylova

Born in Trinidad and Tobago, the son of politician Basil Warrington who died when Don was six, he was raised in Newcastle upon Tyne. At 16, he decided it was time to tell his family that he wanted to be an actor.

'They met my announcement with a degree of surprise because, as far as they could tell, there was no reason for me to want to, beyond the odd school play,' he recalls. 'But I do remember the local bishop thinking that I was quite good, which lead me to believe that if the clergy approved, there must be something in it!'

He joined his local repertory theatre aged 17, where, along the way, he swapped his Geordie accent for the deep, eloquent tone that has become his trade mark and landed him numerous roles and TV voiceovers.

As well as *Rising Damp*, Don has starred as Judge Ken Winyard in *New Street Law*, appeared in *Grange Hill*, *Red Dwarf* and *C.A.T.S. Eyes* and recently played The President of Great Britain in *Doctor Who: Rise of the Cybermen*. He is a regular on the BBC2 series *Grumpy Old Men* and also took over from fellow contestant Cherie Lunghi to star in the ads for a well-known coffee brand, in which he plays a plantation owner. In 2008, he was awarded the MBE (Member of the Order of the British Empire) for his services to drama.

Don is attracted to *Strictly* because of the journey the celebs embark on. 'I love the fact that you can sit back and watch someone, with no dancing experience whatsoever, learn a brand new skill,' he says. 'To me, that's fascinating.'

The 56 year old loves to dance at parties and has had some dance training at drama school but admits 'it was a very long time ago!' He is looking forward to learning ballroom but feels that Latin may come more naturally to him. 'If I'd had the time before I would have learnt Latin and salsa,' he says. 'I love the emotional and sensual language of Latin.'

As a stage actor, Don is used to performing in front of a live audience but he believes appearing on *Strictly* will be completely different. 'I'm not thinking about the show at the moment,' he says. 'I prefer to put all my energy into concentrating on my training sessions with Lilia.'

How big a fan of *Strictly Come Dancing* are you?
Test your knowledge with this fun quiz.

Strictly Quiz

1 Which celebrity kicked off the show in series one with the first-ever *Strictly* dance?

2 Which celebrity came close second to Jill Halfpenny in series two?

3 At which sport did Gabby Logan represent Wales in the 1990 Commonwealth Games?

4 Which judge found himself snookered after being presented with a challenge by Dennis Taylor?

5 Who was the first celebrity to receive a perfect score of 40?

6 Which couple shocked the judges with their unconventional dummy dance?

7 'Hat, why bother? Waltz, why bother?' Which newsreader's ballroom provoked this throw-away line from Craig?

8 Who has achieved the dubious honour of getting the lowest-ever score?

9 What did David Dickinson clench between his teeth for his terrible tango?

10 What disaster befell Lilia in the semi-final of series three, while she danced the samba with Darren Gough?

11 Which veteran pop star turned up to support old pal Gloria Hunniford and told the judges, 'Do not be rude to my Gloria!'?

12 Which couple did Bruno call 'the dominatrix and the rascal'?

13 Which sportsman said, 'I was hugely relieved when I got to the paso doble because at last I can dance like a bloke.'?

14 In series three, which celebrity kissed Craig after he commented, 'Her problem is that she cannot dance at all!'?

15 Apart from modelling, what is Penny Lancaster-Stewart's profession?

16 Which dancer had Len ranting, 'You're an absolute doughnut!' and complaining, 'I don't want this programme to turn into Cirque du Soleil!'

17 Peter Schmeichel's series-four samba started a dance craze around the country. What was the name of his signature move?

18 Who is the youngest *Strictly* contestant to date?

19 Who is the oldest?

20 Whose series-four waltz left Craig 'absolutely mesmerized.'?

21 Who partnered TV chef James Martin?

22 Who stepped in to co-present the show while Tess was off following the birth of her daughter?

23 Which two dances were introduced in series four?

24 Who provides the booming voice-over for the show?

25 Which TV show has starred *Strictly Come Dancing* contestants Stephanie Beacham and Claire King?

26 Which TV personality described herself as a 'little old lady with a hump' when she began her *Strictly Come Dancing* journey?

27 How many snooker players have now taken part in the show?

28 From which other venue, apart from the BBC's London studio, has the show been broadcast?

29 Who is the professional dance partner of Vincent Simone?

30 Who won the 2007 Christmas special with a perfect American smooth?

Jessie Wallace

You can expect plenty of emotion from actress Jessie Wallace in series six – she even cries when she watches it! 'I love all the wicked dresses, the fantastic make-up and the glamour of it all,' she says. 'I love watching all these people learning a new skill and then seeing them perform in front of their families, who end up crying with the emotion, and then I end up crying too!'

Jessie will be right at home in the hair and make-up department as she has a City and Guilds qualification in theatrical make-up and started her career making wigs and putting on the slap at the Royal Shakespeare Company. While there, she became

Partner: Darren Bennett

friends with actor Iain Glen, who encouraged her to apply for drama college The Poor School, from which she graduated in 1999.

A year later, Jessie got her big break after auditioning for a small part in *EastEnders*. She didn't get the role but producers thought she'd be a great addition to the new family about to move into the Square, and sexy, sassy Kat Slater was born.

After five years as a soap icon, Jessie said goodbye to Albert Square and moved on to other television productions such as BBC dramas *A Class Apart*, with Nathaniel Parker, and *The Dinner Party*, with Alison Steadman and Lee Evans, as well as ITV's *Wild at Heart*. She also made her West End theatre debut earlier in 2008, when she replaced Denise van Outen in *Rent Remixed* at the Duke of York Theatre.

The 36 year old, who has a three-year-old daughter named Tallulah, is planning to use her time on the show to get fit. 'I'm so looking forward to seeing how my body changes with the training.'

And, two weeks into training, she was already making fine progress and having tons of fun.

'I thought I had two left feet, but with Darren teaching me, I think I've been picking it up quite quickly – I'm quite surprised at myself!' she admits. 'I always wondered how on earth can you manage to dance and look happy at the same time – but now I know, you can't help but smile because you're having so much fun'!'

Although she has never had dance training before, Jessie is a dance champ in her own right already. When she was ten years old she was in Mallorca where she and a friend entered a dance competition and Jessie won it! She remembers walking away with the rubbish prize – a lion bean bag – and feeling really proud of herself!

Even so, up until now most of the actress's fancy footwork has taken place behind closed doors. 'I put on MTV or one of Tallulah's little mini radios and we jig around to something like Girls Aloud! I've even been practising the salsa in front of her and she's looking at me going, "What are you doing, Mummy?"'

Be Your Own Judge

		Andrew and Ola	Austin and Erin	Cherie and James	Christine and Matthew	Don and Lilia	Gary and Karen	Gillian and Anton	Heather and Brian
Show 1	Your Score								
	Judges' Score								
Show 2	Your Score								
	Judges' Score								
Show 3	Your Score								
	Judges' Score								
Show 4	Your Score								
	Judges' Score								
Show 5	Your Score								
	Judges' Score								
Show 6	Your Score								
	Judges' Score								
Show 7	Your Score								
	Judges' Score								
Show 8	Your Score								
	Judges' Score								
Show 9	Your Score								
	Judges' Score								
Show 10	Your Score								
	Judges' Score								
Show 11	Your Score								
	Judges' Score								
Show 12	Your Score								
	Judges' Score								
Show 13	Your Score								
	Judges' Score								
The Final	Your Score								
	Judges' Score								

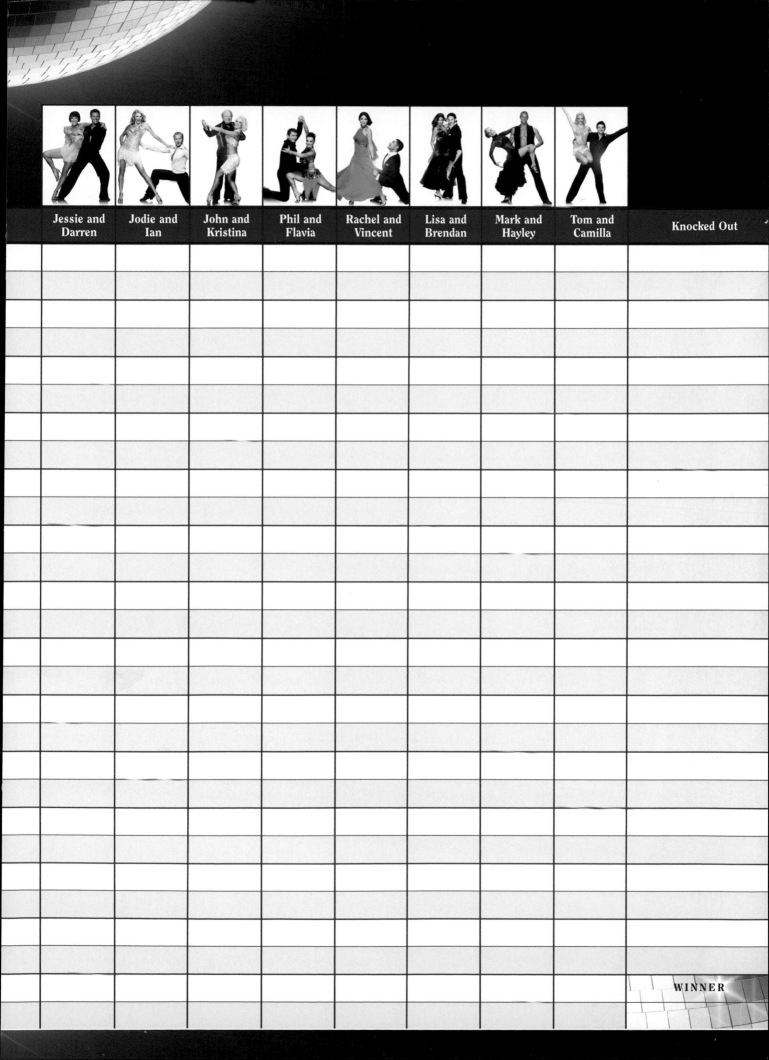

Jessie and Darren	Jodie and Ian	John and Kristina	Phil and Flavia	Rachel and Vincent	Lisa and Brendan	Mark and Hayley	Tom and Camilla	Knocked Out
								WINNER

You Dancin'?

Strictly Come Dancing fans may look forward to their Saturday-night glamour fix but they are no couch potatoes. Since the birth of the show, in 2004, the nation has been in the grip of dance fever and class attendances have swelled.

'A colossal amount of people have taken up classes because of the show,' confirms Len Goodman. Keith Jones, of the British Dance Council, agrees.

'It's been a wonderful programme for the business,' he says. 'The general trend is up since the programme started, and there has definitely been a surge in interest in the ballroom studios.'

Keith, who started his career with Mecca ballrooms, remembers the heyday of ballroom dancing but says that some things never change.

'Fifty years ago, we had 120 ballrooms and every town had a Mecca ballroom,' he says. 'They were very luxuriously fitted and each one reproduced the Fred Astaire–Ginger Rogers atmosphere. But the thing that remains the same is that dancing is at the heart of the boy-meets-girl syndrome.'

As well as a way to meet members of the opposite sex, dancing can bring an established couple closer together.

'A lot of couples do it to solve their marriage problems because it gives them another focus, a way to better themselves, and often makes their relationship better,' says Craig Revel Horwood. 'Many people say they don't want to dance together because they'd end up fighting but, actually, it should be the reverse of that. It's something you can enjoy together.'

Len, who has run dance schools for over 30 years, recommends classes for married and single people of all ages.

'It's such a lovely thing to do, for a couple of reasons,' he comments. 'If you're married or with a partner, it's something you can do together, something you share. If you're single, it's an opportunity to meet other people. I even have people from my dance school who came on their own and have got married.

'As far as your health is concerned, it's good exercise, and in addition to that you're learning to do something. My philosophy is that people are coming for a good time, so that's what we give them. If they learn to dance, that's a bonus. It shouldn't be strict and difficult – I want it to be fun, I want it to be enjoyable. We don't have supermarket lighting; it's all dimmed so you don't feel stupid.'

As an East End lad who worked on the docks, Len came to dancing relatively late, at 19. He still remembers what a daunting experience his first dance class was.

'I was adamant I wasn't going to walk up those stairs and go dancing,' he recalls. 'I had to be dragged in and only agreed when I was told there were loads of girls there. But once I got started, I loved it.'

Even though that was some years ago, Len sympathizes with potential dancers who find the idea of joining a class too traumatic to face.

'The hardest step in dancing is the first step through the door of the dance school,' says Len.

'The biggest thing is that people don't want to look silly but there are a couple of ways to get going. If you don't want to start in a dance class, you can phone up your local dance studio and have half an hour's private lesson, either on your own or with your partner, to see how you get on and whether you like it. Alternatively, you can buy a dance DVD and have a little practice indoors to see if you have any ability and enjoy it.'

Once you've decided to take the plunge and join a group class, choose carefully.

'What puts people off dancing is the fear of failure, but it's not as traumatic as people might imagine and no one is going be humiliated,' advises Len. 'Make sure you go to beginners classes. Look in the local paper or phone the local dance hall and they will tell you when they are. They really are for beginners so everybody is in the same boat. With my beginners classes, you really have to be starting from scratch – you can't come if you can dance a bit!'

In his experience, Len has found that women are naturally more open to the idea of dance classes, but once the men find their dancing feet, the tables are turned.

'Most of the men get dragged along by their wives but once they get going, they want to keep going when some of the wives want to pack it in,' laughs Len. 'They get more hooked than the women, as a general rule. So, if hubby's reluctant, go and have a private lesson and see how you get on.

'Dancing is suitable for all ages and, in my opinion, should be taught in schools.'

Ballrooms and dance halls may not dominate our towns any more but ballroom schools and Latin classes, such as the salsa, are everywhere.

Look at small ads in your local shops, surf the net or look in the phone book and there is bound to be a class near you that will suit your style, so there's never been a better time to start.

Whether it's a Saturday-night entertainment or a hobby, the appeal of dancing is universal and goes back to the beginning of civilization.

'There are very few things that are common in every culture in the world,' says Len. 'But, you could go to the most isolated place in the Brazilian rain forest and find a tribe that has never seen civilization, and there will be people banging on a tree stump, and other people moving around to the beat. There's very little else you can say that about. There has been dancing since the cavemen.'

Professional Passion

It's one thing taking up salsa as a way of shedding the pounds and having some fun, but quite another if you want to be the next James and Ola Jordan. Becoming a professional dancer takes time, effort and a lot of talent and Len's advice is to start young.

'Every kid who comes to dance school wants to be a professional or a dance teacher!' he says 'In fact a very small percentage go on to be dance teachers, and with the vast majority, once they become a certain age,

hormones takes over. Many of them start when they are seven or eight and then they turn into teenagers, get more interested in boyfriends and girlfriends and their dance career is over. But all the teachers in my dance school started out as kids. If you have the talent and want to do it, then go for it.'

Craig agrees that, for those who want to make it their living, the time to start training for the future is now.

'Young people who feel they'd like to be professional should ask their parents to enrol them,' he says. 'If they're already involved in it they need to make sure they train regularly, because that's the most important thing.

'You can't leave it for two weeks and then go once. It's important that it's a regular thing and that you get a really good dance partner. The teaming of partnerships is the thing that can make or break you, and that's why everyone is always looking for great partners.

'Generally, dance teachers are able to steer people in the right direction if they want to take it to a professional level but it's very hard work. It requires an enormous amount of dedication and discipline, and without that you won't make it. The professional dancers who we have on the show are all champions in their own right and that's all due to the fact that they work really hard – they literally train five or six hours a day.'

As a young dancer, former ballroom champion Len put himself through a punishing schedule as he carried on working at the docks while training for competitions. Even as a teacher he struggled to make ends meet.

'The trouble is that you can't earn enough initially as a dance teacher and that's why it gets hard. You may have to have

127

a job, as I did. I worked from seven in the morning to five at night and then I was straight up the dance school, teaching.

'There comes a point where you can't cope and you have to decide between the job and the dance, and then it's a real struggle. You've got to have a passion for dancing and be totally committed. You give up a lot because it's a very unsociable job. Dance schools are open when people finish work, so when your friends are out, you're still working. You have to be really committed.'

While only a few make it to the top, Len says there's fun to be had along the way.

'There's little money in it unless you get to the very top then, like in most things, it can be more lucrative,' he reveals. 'My dad loved gardening and I hate it. To me, digging a garden is work but Dad once said to me, "Work is anything you don't like doing." I've been fortunate that I love dancing and it's what I've done as a job all my life, but I've never considered it work.'

Craig's tips on starting out

1 Buy a good book or DVD because that will give you an insight into the dialogue. The language can flummox you when you first walk in, so a book will help you familiarize yourself with the terminology before you go to a class. That will give you the confidence and you'll be three lessons ahead of everyone else at the beginners class.

2 Always choose a beginners class. Don't over challenge yourself so you get scared off.

3 Go somewhere local, somewhere that you're going to go back to. If you go miles away it won't last long because you won't make the effort.

4 Make sure you wear something comfortable to dance lessons.

5 Once you've got three steps under your belt you can start dancing in public. You can go to any ballroom then and just dance a simple foxtrot. Then you progress and learn more steps until, suddenly, you're really confident and everyone is asking you for lessons.

IMPERIAL SOCIETY OF TEACHERS OF DANCING	NATIONAL ASSOCIATION OF TEACHERS OF DANCING	INTERNATIONAL DANCE TEACHERS ASSOCIATION	UNITED KINGDOM ALLIANCE OF PROFESSIONAL TEACHERS OF DANCING
The ISTD Dance Examinations Board offers dance examinations in 15 dance genres, including Modern Ballroom and Latin American. Teachers who offer their examinations can be found throughout the UK and overseas. If you can't find a teacher in your area they will provide a list of schools, just email: education@istd.org.	The National Association offers classes and examinations in the following branches: Ballroom, Latin American, Disco, Street, Rock 'n' Roll, Country & Western Line Dancing, Salsa, Mambo, Merengue, Classical & Modern Sequence. Contact them for more information.	Log on to their website to find a dance teacher or course near you – all over the world – or contact them direct and they will send you a free and comprehensive list of IDTA-registered teachers in your area.	Log on to their website or contact the UKA direct for guidance on finding your nearest registered dance teacher.
Imperial House 22–26 Paul Street London EC2A 4QE	**NATD** 44–47 The Broadway Thatcham Berkshire RG19 3HP	**International House** 76 Bennett Road Brighton East Sussex BN2 5JL	**Centenary House** 38–40 Station Road Blackpool FY4 1EU
Tel: +44 (0)20 7377 1577 **Website: www.istd.org**	**Tel: + 44 (0) 1635 868888** **Website: www.natd.org.uk**	**Tel: +44 (0)1273 685652** **Website: www.idta.co.uk**	**Tel: +44 (0)1253 408828** **Website: www.ukadance.co.uk**